Ethical Decision Making
for Digital Libraries

CHANDOS
INFORMATION PROFESSIONAL SERIES

Series Editor: Ruth Rikowski
(email: Rikowskigr@aol.com)

Chandos' new series of books are aimed at the busy information professional. They have been specially commissioned to provide the reader with an authoritative view of current thinking. They are designed to provide easy-to-read and (most importantly) practical coverage of topics that are of interest to librarians and other information professionals. If you would like a full listing of current and forthcoming titles, please visit our web site **www.chandospublishing.com** or contact Hannah Grace-Williams on email info@chandospublishing.com or telephone number +44 (0) 1865 884447.

New authors: we are always pleased to receive ideas for new titles; if you would like to write a book for Chandos, please contact Dr Glyn Jones on email gjones@chandospublishing.com or telephone number +44 (0) 1865 884447.

Bulk orders: some organisations buy a number of copies of our books. If you are interested in doing this, we would be pleased to discuss a discount. Please contact Hannah Grace-Williams on email info@chandospublishing.com or telephone number +44 (0) 1865 884447.

Ethical Decision Making for Digital Libraries

Cokie G. Anderson

Chandos Publishing
Oxford • England

Chandos Publishing (Oxford) Limited
Chandos House
5 & 6 Steadys Lane
Stanton Harcourt
Oxford OX29 5RL
UK
Tel: +44 (0) 1865 884447 Fax: +44 (0) 1865 884448
Email: info@chandospublishing.com
www.chandospublishing.com

First published in Great Britain in 2006

ISBN:
1 84334 149 2 (paperback)
1 84334 195 6 (hardback)

British Library Cataloguing-in-Publication Data.
A catalogue record for this book is available from the British Library.

*In memory of my grandmother, Cora Gramling Gaston,
who taught me right from wrong.*

Contents

Acknowledgements

I would like to thank my colleague David C. Maxwell and the Dean of Libraries at Oklahoma State University, Sheila Grant Johnson, without whose assistance and support this book would not have been possible. I am grateful to my family and friends who encouraged me throughout this process, especially Marc Anderson, Stephen Stray, Carol Walker, Richard Sternlof, Gina Minks and Jason Brumley. And my deepest thanks to my sister, Annick Salomon, who patiently read every word of the manuscript and offered invaluable help and advice.

About the author

Cokie G. Anderson is an associate professor at Oklahoma State University and is the Director of the OSU Library Electronic Publishing Center. She received her Masters in Library and Information Science from the University of Oklahoma. She is the co-author with David C. Maxwell of *Starting a Digitisation Center* (Chandos, 2004). She is on the editorial board of *The Electronic Library* and is a frequent presenter at conferences. Many of her presentations may be accessed via her website, *http://digital.library.okstate.edu/cokie.html*.

The author may be contacted at:

E-mail: *cokie.anderson@okstate.edu*

Preface

The idea for this book came to me during a digitisation conference sponsored by the University of Oklahoma in March 2005. The keynote speaker, a historian, was lamenting the fact that in digitising the writings of a great US President, an American university with a highly respected digital library programme had unfortunately used a published version that was considered inaccurate and inferior by historians. The university had chosen that edition because it was in the public domain and no copyright issues would arise. No historians had been consulted or involved in the decision. This scholar was very disturbed that researchers using this online edition, sponsored as it was by a reputable academic institution, would rely on it to the detriment of their own scholarship. He charged those of us in attendance, most of whom work in academic or research libraries, to consider carefully the responsibility we bore for the materials we made available online, and to digitise only the best version of any given work. This struck me as an issue that was not really dealt with in the professional codes of ethics for librarians. Most codes with which I was familiar focused on issues of access and confidentiality. The unique ethical dilemmas that face digital librarians in selecting, preparing, preserving and publishing digital materials are not addressed. I wrote this book in hopes of stimulating discussion of these issues in professional organisations, graduate schools of information science, and among librarians who work in this field. Many of our professional codes have not been updated since the advent of the Internet; considering the impact this innovation had and continues to have on our profession, it seems time to correct that oversight.

Writing a book on ethics is fraught with dangers, not the least of which are self-righteousness and arrogance. I do not wish to be guilty of moral imperialism, and I recognise that the book will inevitably reflect biases that arise from my education in the Western philosophical tradition. This book is intended to make people think about these issues and to spur discussion of professional ethics for librarians in the digital age, not to dictate the behaviour of others. I hope the reader finds it useful.

An introduction to ethical theory and applied ethics

Ethics, or moral philosophy, seeks to understand and explain the nature of morality, to provide a theory of right and wrong (Waluchow, 2003). Substantive ethics, also called normative ethics, 'aim[s] to formulate standards of correctness for evaluation and decision' (Mautner, 1999). It is in this category that the major schools of ethical thought – the virtue ethics of Aristotle, the categorical imperative of Kant, and the utilitarianism of Mill and Bentham – fall. Applied ethics, which includes professional ethics, is a subcategory of normative ethics that attempts to apply the principles and standards of moral thought to guide us in everyday decisions.

Which principles should we rely upon in making our moral decisions? Aristotle's virtue ethics ask 'What should I be?' rather than 'What should I do?' The focus is on developing a good moral character rather than merely following rules. Deontological theories, such as Kant's categorical imperative, are primarily concerned with the intent of the actor rather than the consequences of the action. Utilitarianism and related teleological theories are concerned instead with outcomes and consequences. One's basic obligation, in this school of thought, is to minimise bad outcomes and maximise good ones. However, it does not allow decisions based on the outcome alone; one must also ask whether the action itself is moral. These schools of thought have all contributed important principles to the field of applied and professional ethics.

Virtue ethics

One of the earliest works on ethics in Western philosophy is Aristotle's *Nicomachean Ethics*. In this work Aristotle (384–322 BCE) sets forth his theory of virtue, which he defines as a disposition to choose well. Happiness is the ultimate goal, but Aristotle defines happiness as 'activity in accordance with virtue' not as 'pleasant amusements' (Bk. X: Ch. 7). By exercising the moral virtues of courage, temperance, generosity, truth and justice, and the intellectual virtues of science, art, practical wisdom, intuitive reason and philosophical wisdom, one finds happiness. Virtue is something we learn by doing, like an art, and there are no hard and fast rules to guide us. One must try to do what a 'person of practical reason' would do in the circumstances, always choosing the mean between the extremes of excess and deficiency. Although Aristotle stresses our autonomy as moral agents, he is a consequentialist in judging the rightness of actions based on their results. He takes into account that there will be different perspectives, and that different people will make different decisions, based upon what they believe to be reasonable.

Kant and deontological theory

In deontological theory, an act is judged by its intent and inherent morality, regardless of its consequences. Immanuel

Kant (1724–1804), the primary theorist in this area, saw reason as the basis of morality. He stated his categorical imperative thus: 'I ought never to act except in such a way that I can also will that my maxim should be a universal law of nature' (Waluchow, 2003). This is a lofty sentiment, but as a practical guide for behaviour is somewhat paralysing. Can one truly look at every action and honestly say one would want the motivating principle behind it to be a universal law of nature? Most would find this intimidating, to say the least.

Kant also focused on the rights of the individual, especially the freedom to choose for oneself. This right to choose may be expanded to include the right to know the truth, the right to privacy, the right to be free from harm, and the right to expect others to live up to their agreements (Velasquez et al., 1996). Kant requires that one consider not only whether one would wish one's personal rules of behaviour to become universal law, but also to ask oneself if this action will degrade, use or violate the autonomy of another rational being, including oneself. The philosopher R. M. Hare interpreted Kant's universal moral principle to be a maxim that you would be willing for others to rely upon when you are on the receiving end of their actions. This is the theoretical underpinning to the Golden Rule, which exhorts us to 'Do unto others as you would have them do unto you' (Waluchow, 2003).

The great problem with Kant's theory is its inflexibility. There are no exceptions, and no weighing of the relative merits of outcomes. For example, under deontological theory, someone hiding a Jew from the Nazis would be obliged, if asked, to tell the Gestapo where this person was, because lying is immoral. Even though the lie would be for a good reason, it would still violate the moral principle. This strictness can result in the wrong result for the right reason.

Utilitarianism

Utilitarianism is the primary teleological theory. Developed by Jeremy Bentham (1748–1832) and John Stuart Mill (1806–73), it rejects the idea that there is a natural order or divine law and instead relies on an objective, universal standard of good: utility. The good of an action may be judged by its consequences, and thus its 'utility,' or value, to society. Mill and Bentham agreed with the hedonists that happiness is the ultimate utility; pain is bad and pleasure is good. Therefore, the ethical decision is one that leads to consequences that produce happiness and minimise pain. It should be stressed that in utilitarianism, it is not one's own happiness that is the ultimate value and moral compass, but the happiness of all concerned, all of whom count equally. The concern for what is best for everyone leads to a weakness in utilitarian theory: how does one know what is best for others? To say that I know what is best for you is presumptuous at best and paternalistic at worst. The best one can do is to put oneself in the other's place, but that does not overcome inherent personal biases. Within utilitarianism, there are act utilitarianism and rule utilitarianism. In act utilitarianism, each particular act is judged by its own consequences rather than by any outside standard. In rule utilitarianism, there is an effort to develop a set of rules that, when obeyed, will generally maximise utility. The difficulty with rule utilitarianism arises first with promulgating rules that can cover a wide variety of situations, and then with becoming more focused on rules than on moral actions. A danger in both act and rule utilitarianism is getting the right result but getting it in the wrong way. An action can have positive results and still be immoral. One may steal to help the poor, but stealing is still wrong.

G. E. Moore attempted to give consideration to theories of value other than happiness with his pluralistic theory of value, preference utilitarianism. He proposed other things of ultimate, irreducible value in addition to happiness: knowledge, beauty, and friendship. Under his theory, an act is good when it satisfies people's preferences. This seems to offer more flexibility by allowing consideration of something other than happiness as the ultimate good, although people's preferences will, of course, differ. In addition, how does one determine what people's preferences are, whose preferences should be given the most weight, and how the greatest number of preferences can be satisfied?

Summary

The above text provides a very brief overview of the major schools of thought in ethics, and is by no means a detailed and thoughtful examination of ethical theory. The purpose is to provide the reader with basic knowledge of the foundations underpinning the professional ethics that will be examined in the remainder of this book. Each of these theories has its strengths and weaknesses, its detractors and adherents. We can learn something from all of them to apply to the ethical decisions we face in our own lives. The truth of one theory does not take away from that of another. As John Stuart Mill stated in *On Liberty*, 'conflicting doctrines, instead of one being true and the other false, share the truth between them, and the [one] is needed to supply the remainder of the truth of which the [other] embodies only a part' (Waluchow, 2003).

2

Professional codes of ethics in the information professions

The American Library Association (ALA) enacted its Code of Ethics in 1938, making it the first such code of professional conduct in the information professions (Trushina, 2004). The ALA Code (ALA, 1995) expresses the following 'broad statements to guide ethical decision making':

- We provide the highest level of service to all library users through appropriate and usefully organised resources; equitable service policies; equitable access; and accurate, unbiased, and courteous responses to all requests.

- We uphold the principles of intellectual freedom and resist all efforts to censor library resources.

- We protect each library user's right to privacy and confidentiality with respect to information sought or received and resources consulted, borrowed, acquired or transmitted.

- We recognise and respect intellectual property rights.

- We treat co-workers and other colleagues with respect, fairness and good faith, and advocate conditions of employment that safeguard the rights and welfare of all employees of our institutions.

- We do not advance private interests at the expense of library users, colleagues, or our employing institutions.

- We distinguish between our personal convictions and professional duties and do not allow our personal beliefs to interfere with fair representation of the aims of our institutions or the provision of access to their information resources.

- We strive for excellence in the profession by maintaining and enhancing our own knowledge and skills, by encouraging the professional development of co-workers, and by fostering the aspirations of potential members of the profession.

The first four statements deal with obligations to patrons and society, the last four with obligations to colleagues and the profession. Overall, they show more influence from the virtue ethics of Aristotle (who do we want to be?) and the deontological theory of Kant than with the 'greatest good for the greatest number' principles of utilitarianism. On intellectual freedom and privacy issues in particular, ALA is quite absolutist, defending these principles without exception. This is the cause of much ongoing controversy in the USA on issues ranging from filters on Internet access and the appropriateness of materials dealing with issues of sexuality, to the government's rights to access to patron's library records. ALA has been a leading opponent of those sections of the USA PATRIOT Act 2001 that would permit federal investigators to see library records of patrons' reading materials and Internet use. Some see this as helping terrorists by protecting their privacy; in an opinion piece in *The Washington Times*, Deroy Murdock (2005) denounced ALA's opposition to the Act: 'These dangerously naive or clandestinely seditious librarians are beyond foolish. They potentially jeopardise American lives'. ALA maintains that allowing federal authorities access to any patron's records puts all patrons' privacy in jeopardy. ALA has also defended challenges to books ranging from *The Anarchist's Cookbook*, a guide to making bombs, to Mark Twain's classic *Huckleberry Finn*. ALA also encourages its members to resist all attempts to filter access to the Internet, a policy that has caused many librarians to run afoul of library boards, politicians, and some citizens. Almost all American public libraries now provide patrons with free access to the Web (Ruethling, 2005), and battles over issues of privacy and intellectual freedom have become even more intense in the electronic age.

The codes of ethics/conduct of professional associations in the UK and France have a more utilitarian approach. The Chartered Institute of Library and Information Professionals (CILIP) in the UK stresses responsibility to the 'public good', a very utilitarian concept that is part of its Royal Charter. Members are exhorted to remember that they serve 'society at large', not just the individual customer, and to 'consider the public good', especially as it concerns 'vulnerable groups'. The CILIP document sets forth 12 ethical principles on which the code of professional practice is based (CILIP, 2004):

The conduct of members should be characterised by the following general principles, presented here in no particular order of priority:

1. Concern for the public good in all professional matters, including respect for diversity within society, and the promoting of equal opportunities and human rights.

2. Concern for the good reputation of the information profession.

3. Commitment to the defence, and the advancement,

of access to information, ideas and works of the imagination.

4. Provision of the best possible service within available resources.

5. Concern for balancing the needs of actual and potential users and the reasonable demands of employers.

6. Equitable treatment of all information users.

7. Impartiality, and avoidance of inappropriate bias, in acquiring and evaluating information and in mediating it to other information users.

8. Respect for confidentiality and privacy in dealing with information users.

9. Concern for the conservation and preservation of our information heritage in all formats.

10. Respect for, and understanding of, the integrity of information items and for the intellectual effort of those who created them.

11. Commitment to maintaining and improving personal professional knowledge, skills and competences.

12. Respect for the skills and competences of all others, whether information professionals or information users, employers or colleagues.

'Commitment to the defence ... of access to information' is a far more moderate statement than ALA's 'resist all efforts to censor library resources'. While this may be attributed to differences in temperament and mode of expression in American and British societies, it seems to reflect a fundamental difference in underlying philosophy, the Kantian principle above all considerations versus the utilitarian concern for overall public good. The UK-based Library Association's Code of Conduct states, 'Members should not knowingly promote material the prime purpose of which is to encourage discrimination on the grounds of race, colour, creed, gender or sexual orientation' (Library Association, 1983). Le Code de Déontologie du Bibliothécaire de L'Association des Bibliothécaires Français, while instructing librarians to 'exercise no censorship whatsoever, guaranteeing the pluralism and intellectual encyclopaedism of the collections' and to 'facilitate the free circulation of information', also reminds its members to 'enforce the laws and rules concerning the collections, as well as the law decisions, notably those forbidding the promotion of all kind of discrimination and violence, without substituting himself to the law' (ABF, 2003). In contrast, the ALA's Freedom to Read Statement (ALA, 1953–2004) asserts that:

> It is in the public interest for publishers and librarians to make available the widest diversity of views and expressions, including those that are unorthodox, unpopular, or considered dangerous by the majority ... It is not in the public interest to force a reader to accept the prejudgment of a label characterising any expression or its author as subversive or dangerous.

In addition:

> It is the responsibility of publishers and librarians, as guardians of the people's freedom to read, to contest encroachments upon that freedom by individuals or groups seeking to impose their own standards or tastes upon the community at large; and by the government whenever it seeks to reduce or deny public access to public information.

Despite the repeated references to the 'public interest' it is not the utilitarian concern for maximising public good that is at work here, but the Kantian respect for autonomy of the individual: 'Americans do not need others to do their thinking for them' (Ibid.).

The IFLA website (IFLA, 2005) presents the codes of professional ethics/conduct of various library organisations worldwide. The codes generally cover the same ground: high standards of service, avoidance of conflicts of interest and bias, professional development, respect for intellectual property, and devotion to intellectual freedom and patron privacy. These last tend to be the primary concern of the codes (Trushina, 2004) and of discussions about ethics in the information professions. Certainly the digital environment raises new concerns in the area of privacy. Access to personal information has become a major concern; there have been security breaches of credit card company computers and database vendors by hackers. In addition to protecting the privacy of patron reading habits and information requests, librarians must now be concerned that the personal information we have always collected on library users – names, addresses, contact information, ID numbers – is adequately protected from those who would seek to misuse it. In this area, we may look for guidance to codes of ethics for those who work with information technology. The Association of Computing Machinery Code of Ethics and Professional Conduct (1992) observes that 'technology enables the collection and exchange of personal information on a scale unprecedented in ... history ... [T]here is increased potential for violating the privacy of individuals and groups'. The code requires IT professionals to ensure that the data are accurate and protected from falling into the hands of others. This is to be accomplished in part by collecting the minimum amount of personal data necessary and by establishing and enforcing retention and disposal policies.

The digital world increases concerns about intellectual property rights, especially for those who are involved in digitisation. The Internet started out as a sort of commune where no one worried too much about copyright, ownership and piracy – everything was shared by everyone. Intellectual property issues have now become major concerns. For anyone engaged in a digitisation project, the first question must be, do we have the rights to publish this? If the material is in the public domain (determined by the law of the country in which the electronic publication will take place), it is safe to proceed. Otherwise, the information professional has a duty to make sure they have permission from the copyright holder to publish an online version. This is an ethical duty as well as a legal one; our codes of ethics all express a respect for the intellectual property right of others. In the digital world, intellectual property issues can be hazy. Are images or clip art copyrighted? What are the terms of use if they are not explicitly stated on the website? Once again, the IT profession has addressed this ethical issue. The ACM Code of Ethics and Professional Conduct specifically prohibits 'tak[ing] credit for other's ideas or work, even in cases where the work has not been explicitly protected by copyright, patent, etc'.

Intellectual property issues also arise when licensing content from vendors. In the past, if a library discontinued a print journal subscription, or if publication ceased for whatever reason, access to past issues was not interrupted. Now, however, many libraries are switching to electronic-only access to journals, and some journals are appearing solely in digital form. This raises the question of what happens if the library stops subscribing or the publisher stops publishing. Is access to past issues ended? What are the rights and obligations of digital libraries in this situation? Librarians believe they must preserve ongoing access to these materials, and are taking steps to archive electronic materials in several ways. The LOCKSS Program (Lots Of Copies Keep Stuff Safe) is working with publishers to build a preservation framework for electronic journals (*http://lockss.stanford.edu*). In the LOCKSS model, continued access is ensured by creating and maintaining multiple copies of digital journals on servers at participating institutions. If something happens to the materials on one server, copies will still exist on other servers in other locations. However, LOCKSS can only store copies of journals if the publisher gives permission to do so, and some publishers view these efforts as a threat to their business or a violation of digital journal licences. Another method for preserving access to electronic journal articles is by archiving copies of articles written by researchers at one's institution in an institutional repository. This allows authors to archive their own works and provides alternative access to materials but does not ensure long-term access to complete journals.

The American Society for Information Science and Technology (ASIS&T), which despite its name is international in scope and membership, includes professionals who are librarians, information technology professionals, educators and information scientists, and who work primarily in corporate or academic settings. The ASIS&T Professional Guidelines recognise 'the diversity of goals or objectives, sometimes conflicting, among producers, vendors, mediators, and users of information systems'. Professionals are advised to provide access to information 'freely ... subject to restraints of producers, vendors and employers' (ASIS&T, 1992).

Preservation is an area that is not always addressed by library associations' codes of professional ethics, but it is one of the most pressing issues in the digital library world. The CILIP Ethical Principles, updated in 2004, do mention 'Concern for the conservation and preservation of our information heritage *in all formats* [italics mine]'. Older codes of ethics (ALA updated 1995; the Library Association, 1983) did not include obligations to conserve or preserve materials, probably because this was considered the purview of the archivist. If we look to the codes of ethics of archivists' organisations, preservation is a prime concern. The Code of Ethics for Archivists promulgated by the Society of American Archivists (1992) places a premium on preserving and protecting the integrity of 'documentary materials of long-term value', noting in the accompanying commentary that such materials are covered regardless of the 'physical format in which they are recorded'. Under this code, archivists must collaborate to make sure materials are in a safe repository where they are both accessible and properly cared for. To ensure the preservation of materials, the Code recognises the need for archivists to work together to formulate and promulgate professional standards, and it requires members to keep current on standards and best practices and to follow the highest standards possible in their work. Digital librarians likewise must work to establish widely adopted standards and must adhere to them when creating their own electronic files. Standards are essential to long-term preservation of digital objects, and the development, dissemination of, and adherence to standards is an ethical obligation for digital librarians.

The archivists' code also raises privacy concerns of a new kind: the privacy rights of those mentioned in archival records. Other codes of ethics have focused on the privacy rights of clients and patrons, but digitisation of materials adds this new area of concern for privacy rights. Suppose a donor deposits personal papers with an institution, and in doing so explicitly gives the institution permission to digitise their correspondence and publish it on the Web. The donor is aware of what will be done and has waived their right to privacy; they want these letters to be read by the world. But what of their correspondents and those mentioned in the letters? What of their right to privacy? The Code of Ethics for Archivists states, 'Archivists respect the privacy of individuals who created, or are the subjects of, documentary materials of long-term value, *especially those who had no voice in the disposition of the materials* [italics mine]'. Archive professionals are advised to recommend that donors take steps to protect the privacy of third parties. Archivists will sometimes suggest that donors restrict access to the collection for a period of time, usually long enough to make sure those mentioned in the documents in question are deceased. Alternatively, they may seek permission of the third parties before making the materials openly available, particularly if they contemplate publishing them online. This goes against the grain for librarians who are trained to resist all restrictions on access to information. In the world of digitisation, however, similar precautions may be necessary to protect the privacy of the individuals involved and to protect digital libraries from lawsuits.

As we look for ethical guidelines for digital libraries, we will find much that is helpful in the codes established by archivists and by information technology professionals. The ASIS&T Professional Guidelines urge members to 'resist...inappropriate selection and acquisitions policies', something that is vital in the field of digitisation, where we must select so carefully because we must use our limited resources wisely. The ACM Code of Ethics and Professional Conduct emphasises the responsibilities of those with specialised knowledge that their co-workers may not share. The general moral imperatives outlined therein oblige members to 'contribute to society and human well being' and, like doctors, to 'avoid harm to others'. The latter section notes that '[w]ell intentioned actions may lead to harm unexpectedly', and advises computing professionals 'to carefully consider potential impacts on all those affected by decisions made during design and implementation'. This is good advice for all of us who design websites or purchase software intended to facilitate access to information, as is the requirement that professionals '[e]nsure that users and those who will be affected by a system have their needs clearly articulated during the assessment and design of requirements'. The code also requires computing professionals to 'minimise malfunctions by following generally accepted standards'. They must also be open and honest about system or software limitations, and must refuse assignments that cannot be completed properly. There is an 'obligation to accept personal accountability for professional work'. Professional ethics may even outweigh legal considerations; computing professionals must 'know and respect existing laws pertaining to professional work' while recognising that 'sometimes existing laws and rules may be immoral or inappropriate and, therefore, must be challenged'.

As we examine the ethical issues facing digital libraries in the coming chapters, we will return to these codes of professional ethics for guidance. The codes are all available online:

- American Library Association (1995) *Code of Ethics*: *http://www.ala.org/ala/oif/statementspols/codeofethics/ codeethics.htm.*

- American Library Association (2004) *Freedom to Read Statement*: *http://www.ala.org/ala/oif/statementspols/ ftrstatement/freedomreadstatement.htm.*

- American Society for Information Science and Technology (1992) *ASIS&T Professional Guidelines*: *http:// www.asis.org/AboutASIS/professional-guidelines.html.*

- Association for Computing Machinery (1992) *ACM Code of Ethics and Professional Conduct*: *http://www.acm.org/constitution.code.html*.

- Chartered Institute of Library and Information Professionals (2004) *Ethical Principles and Code of Professional Practice for Library and Information Professionals* (updated): *http://www.cilip.org.uk/professionalguidance/ethics/*.

- IFLA (2005) *Professional Codes of Ethics/Conduct*. Collection of codes from library associations worldwide: *http://www.ifla.org/faife/ethics/codes.htm*.

- Library Association (1983) *The Library Association's Code of Professional Conduct*: *http://www.la-hq.org.uk/directory/about/conduct.html*.

- Society of American Archivists (1992) *Code of Ethics for Archivists*: *http://www.archivists.org/governance/handbook/app_ethics.asp*.

3

Ethics and digitisation policies

The first and most important way to incorporate ethics into a digitisation policy is to have a written digitisation policy. The thought and discussion that go into actually writing a digitisation policy encourage careful consideration of the institution's principles, especially those underlying its decision to engage in digitisation efforts. When deciding to commit significant resources to a long-term endeavour, an institution has an ethical responsibility to examine the way this undertaking fits with its overall mission. In formulating a digitisation policy, administrators must ask themselves: (1) why are they developing a digitisation policy, and (2) what part will digitisation play in both fulfilling the mission of the institution and in meeting the needs of the institution's primary stakeholders.

Sometimes libraries or library administrators might be tempted to get into digitisation because everyone else is doing it, and no one wants their library to miss out on a major trend. Keeping up with rivals (a particular problem in American university libraries) is not a good reason to jump into digitisation without coming up with a plan and policy first. Administrators should ask themselves the following questions:

■ What is our mission?

- Whom do we serve?

- How will digitisation help us fulfil our mission and meet the needs of those we serve?

- Is digitisation the best way to meet these needs?

- What do we want to digitise? Why do we want to digitise it? Is there a real need/demand to have these materials in electronic form?

- Do we have the expertise to do this properly? If not, are we willing and able to expend the funds necessary to acquire it?

- How are we going to pay for digitisation?

- Is it the best use of our resources?

- Will other important services suffer if we divert resources to digitisation efforts?

- Are we willing and able to make a long-term commitment to maintaining these digitised materials?

- Do we need to do the work ourselves, or is there another institution or consortium we can work with to digitise our materials?

Honest answers to these questions can help a library determine whether digitisation is the right direction to take. Digitisation is not the right answer for every institution, and nothing could be more unethical than diverting scarce resources into a digitisation programme without a plan for utilising those resources efficiently and effectively. A digitisation programme consists of more than buying equipment, scanning materials and putting them online. It is a complicated journey into unknown territory that requires a trustworthy map to guide the traveller. A well-considered digitisation plan can serve as such a map.

Almost all libraries of any size have a mission statement and a collection policy that set forth, among other things, the institution's ethical obligations to its patrons: access to information, privacy of personal records, stewardship of information, and diversity of materials and viewpoints. A digitisation policy should address similar concerns and obligations of digital libraries:

- statement of mission, guiding principles and primary audience;

- accessibility:
  - ensuring online materials are accessible to the disabled;
  - making digitised materials available for no or low cost;

- types of materials to be digitised (formats, priorities, content, subject areas);

- adherence to standards and best practices;

- sustainability:
  - long-term access, preservation, migration;
  - funding;

- intellectual property concerns.

A digitisation policy should address overall guiding principles rather than specifics; details can be covered elsewhere. The National Library of Australia's digitisation policy (NLA, year unknown) is an excellent example of what such a document should be. In its introduction, the NLA defines its role in providing information to Australians through a variety of methods, with an increasing emphasis on electronic delivery of resources to residents in all parts of the nation. The policy goes on to outline the Library's digitisation goals, principles, material to be digitised, digitisation selection criteria, access to digitised collections, approaches to digitisation, management of digitised collections, standards, preservation of original materials, provisions for public consultation, marketing and promotion, coordinating and reporting, and policy review.

The digitisation goals listed include enabling users anywhere to access 'digitised materials relating to Australia and Australians'; 'promoting an understanding of ... the Australian Experience'; working collaboratively with other institutions to compile 'a critical mass of digital items in particular subjects and formats'; and digitising 'rare and fragile collections' to increase accessibility and to help preserve the originals from wear and tear. These statements tell the reader exactly where the Library's priorities lie, and where its efforts will be concentrated. As is appropriate for a national library, the focus will be on Australia and its citizens, both in terms of materials digitised and primary audience. There is also a stated commitment to collaboration on digital projects and to increasing knowledge and understanding of Australia and its culture around the world. It is clear from these goals that a commitment to access is a leading value for this institution. The goals are followed by principles, which 'provide a foundation for the Library's digitisation activities':

- enhancing access to materials and preparing digital surrogates of rare and fragile items to aid in preservation of the originals;

- giving the highest priority to materials 'relating to Australia and Australians';

- making digitisation activities part of routine library activities;

- selecting materials to be digitised in accordance with agreed criteria;

- complying with the Copyright Act;

- focusing on unique material rather than trying to digitise everything;

- scanning materials only once and maintaining a master copy for production of derivative files;

- following library policies on 'access and user charging';

- being responsive to the needs of users, including taking digitisation requests;

- committing to the care and preservation of original materials;

- seeking to work collaboratively with other institutions to minimise any duplication of efforts;

- Ensuring that digital versions accurately represent originals by refraining from manipulation of images.

These principles reflect many of the sentiments expressed in information professionals' codes of ethics, and they reflect a practical and utilitarian approach, focusing on the greatest good for the greatest number.

When it comes to selecting materials for digitisation, the National Library plan first considers 'pragmatic considerations' such as the cost and expertise required for digitisation and the copyright status of the material. Priority is given to materials in the public domain due to the costs of determining and acquiring intellectual property rights. Selection criteria are divided by purpose: to enhance access, to aid in preservation of originals, to increase utility of materials, to provide context for other collections or to fulfil an 'institutional imperative'. The last category includes two types of projects: (1) projects to digitise heavily-used materials to improve efficiency, and (2) projects that might attract funding or income or that might 'promote additional digitisation activities'. The selection criteria also permit the Library to undertake digitisation of materials for other agencies or individuals who would pay the Library for the cost of digitisation.

The Library's policy regarding access to digital collections reflects the values held dear in the profession and enshrined in its codes of ethics. The Library seeks to provide the 'widest possible access' by providing user-friendly navigation, finding aids, simple and advanced search interfaces, and high-quality indexing and metadata. This section does not directly address access issues of cost, although previous mention was made of keeping user charges to minimum. There is no mention at all of making the site accessible and navigable for users with specials needs – the blind who use screen readers and the disabled who need to be able to navigate a website without having to use a mouse. While this may be included under the broad statement of ensuring widest possible access, it would be a good idea and a strong ethical statement to make a written commitment to accessibility for users with special needs. In the USA, state and federally supported sites, including public universities and government agencies, are required by law to comply with the accessibility requirements of s.508 of the Americans with Disabilities Act 1990. The World Wide Web Consortium (W3C) has established the Web Accessibility Initiative (W3C, 2005a) to encourage web developers to design accessible sites. Their 'Introduction to Web Accessibility' (W3C, 2005b) explains their core beliefs: (1) an accessible Web is essential to equal access and equal opportunities for people with disabilities, and (2) everyone benefits from an accessible Web. The Web Accessibility Initiative (WAI) does not decree that there is a moral obligation to make websites accessible, but there is certainly an ethical underpinning to their arguments. WAI encourages a strong sense of social responsibility, and appeals to the virtue ethics question of who we want to be. They make statements that are hard to dispute, such as:

> The Web is an increasingly important resource in many aspects of life: education, employment, government, commerce, health care, recreation, and more. It is essential that the Web be accessible in order to provide *equal access* and *equal opportunity* to people with disabilities. An accessible Web can also help people with disabilities more actively participate in society. [Emphasis in original]

WAI includes a guide for web developers who need to convince corporate bosses that Web accessibility is a smart business decision: 'Developing a Web Accessibility Business Case for Your Organisation' (W3C, 2005c). WAI argues that everyone benefits from adherence to accessibility guidelines: individuals with disabilities, who will have better access to information than they have ever had from any other medium; those, like older users with diminishing abilities, who will also be served by accessibility; general users, who will benefit from the flexibility of accessible web design; and businesses, who will gain a previously untapped customer base by making their sites accessible to all. WAI develops and publishes guidelines and techniques that are considered the standard recommendation for Web accessibility (*http://www.w3.org/WAI/guid-tech*). The Authoring Tool Accessibility Guidelines (ATAG) promulgated by WAI assist developers in evaluating software used for web design. There are links to ATAG evaluations of popular authoring software (*http://www.w3.org/WAI/AU/2002/tools*). The WAI site also provides links to software tools for evaluating and repairing accessibility problems in your web pages (*http://www.w3.org/WAI/ER/existingtools*). Free online utilities, such as Watchfire's WebXACT (*http://Webxact.watchfire.com/*), will check single web pages for compliance with the W3C Web Content Accessibility Guidelines.

From an ethical point of view, a digitisation policy also needs to include a discussion of standards, preservation and sustainability, as the National Library of Australia policy does. As the policy notes, digital preservation and long-term access to digital collections depend on the use of internationally recognised standards. Where there are no formally established standards, the policy directs adherence to international best practice. Conforming to recognised standards and best practices in digitisation is an ethical obligation for digital librarians, just as 'minimis[ing] malfunctions by following generally accepted standards for system design and testing' is required of computer professionals in the Association for Computing Machinery (ACM) Code of Ethics (ACM, 1992). The ACM includes this directive in the section on the moral imperative to 'Avoid harm to others'. It is important that a dedication to standards for the purposes of preservation and long-term access should be expressed in a digitisation policy, but the NLA is also quite correct to avoid naming specific standards and best practices, as these will certainly change. The Library's policy does not address additional aspects of digital preservation, such as migration and sustainable funding. While an institution would ideally have a separate preservation policy that could be referenced in its digitisation policy, it would be wise at least to make a written commitment for the institution to preserve the digital collection over time though adequate funding and planned refreshment, migration and maintenance of digital objects.

In the rush to make digital surrogates of unique materials available online, it is important to remember the ethical obligation to 'do no harm' to the original objects. Funding for digitisation should not come at the cost of funding for preservation for the originals. While digitisation may lower the costs of conservation by reducing the wear and tear on originals, there must still be a commitment by the institution to maintain and preserve the original materials, for no digital surrogate can ever replace them. The NLA reflects this philosophy in its digitisation policy, calling for appropriate steps to be taken to ensure originals are not harmed in the digitisation process and for continued preservation of originals for which there are digital versions.

An interesting aspect of the NLA's digitisation policy is its provisions for public consultation, which require that the Library periodically consult with users about the materials to be digitised and the methods of access available. This is an important acknowledgment of our responsibility to our users – for whose benefit, ostensibly, these collections are being digitised – and reminds us that we have an obligation to be responsive to their needs. There is also a duty to make potential users aware of the digital collections available to them. It is not true that 'if you build it, they will come'; no one can come visit collections they don't know exist. The NLA calls for a marketing plan in its digitisation policy, employing a 'range of strategies'. Inclusion of marketing in the digitisation policy emphasises its importance to projects and functions as a reminder to project managers of the need to publicise their work, whether through announcements on e-mail lists, links on the library homepage, presentations at conferences or articles in newsletters or journals. The more you make users aware of your collections, the more good your collections can potentially do.

Ideally, every institution engaged in digitisation activities would have a carefully considered, thoughtful, well-crafted digitisation policy like that of the National Library of Australia. In reality, not every institution will be able to meet this ideal. Any number of factors may make it unfeasible:

lack of staff or time to devote to such an endeavour; the bureaucracy of large institutions that encumbers adoption of formal policies; the general inefficiency and ineffectiveness of committees; a lack of will or interest on the part of administrators, from whom such policy-setting initiatives must come; or a lack of power and influence on the part of the librarians, archivists and technicians on the frontlines of digitisation who recognise the need for such a policy, but have no means of getting one in place. Most of us will be lucky to get an agreed-upon mission statement for our digitisation policies. While we may not be able to effect a written digitisation policy that has the imprimatur of the administration, we can write down policies for ourselves that address the important ethical considerations of digitisation and that can act as guidelines when questions arise. There may be no mechanism of enforcing these policies, but at least we will have thought out our own priorities and ideals in such a way that we can quickly marshal our thoughts and provide a response to questions or inappropriate or unwise directions from above.

4

Ethics in selection of materials to digitise

Everyone who works in digitisation can agree that there is simply not enough funding to digitise and maintain everything that we would like to have in electronic format. Enhanced accessibility and preservation of originals are the primary motivators for digitising materials. Limited funding requires setting priorities that take these factors into account. Ethical obligations in selecting materials include: (1) establishing criteria that help to prioritise digital projects; (2) respecting the intellectual property rights of the creator or owner of the materials and ensuring that copyright laws are not violated; and (3) taking privacy rights of individuals into account, especially those of third parties who had no say in the disclosure of information.

Priorities and selection criteria

One ethical way to determine which digital projects should be undertaken first is to employ the medical practice of triage, giving first priority to the most fragile, unstable or endangered materials. When employing digitisation as part of a preservation strategy, it is important to focus on the condition of the originals. Those deteriorating most rapidly must be dealt with first, especially audio and video materials. Depending on the materials used to manufacture film or tape and the age of the items, there may be only one chance to play the analogue version and capture it in digital format. Some items may require obsolete equipment not easily available in order to play back the film or tape. Deteriorating materials in obsolete formats should be given a high priority for digitisation, and the services of a professional reformatting service should be employed. Nothing could be more unethical than to destroy a unique recording in an effort to save money by doing the work in-house rather than outsourcing to a professional. Digitisation professionals must work closely with conservators and preservation experts to ensure that no harm is done to original materials in the digitisation process. Manuscripts also require the attention of a conservator before they can be scanned or digitally photographed, as some documents can be damaged by exposure to the bright lights of scanners or digital photography. A professional conservator can make recommendations for protecting the original during the digitisation process, and can provide or recommend training for digitisation staff in handling fragile documents. Choice of equipment and technique is important; overhead scanners, digital cameras and book cradles cause less stress on old or tightly bound books, and filters can protect delicate photographs or papers from being damaged by the scanner or photographer's lights. As stated by John F. Dean in *Digital Imaging and Conservation: Model Guidelines*: 'Every digital imaging project concerned with the capture of artifacts must involve the preservation of the digital image *and* the original artifact and, at the very least, *digitisation should do no harm to the original source document* [Emphasis mine]' (Dean, 2003). We must also bear in mind that while digitisation can be a *part* of a preservation strategy, it 'must

not be viewed as a substitute for other preservation activities'
(Morris, 2005). Digitisation's contribution to preservation
is the reduction in handling and wear and tear on original
items, as most researchers will be able to use the electronic
version. Use of digital surrogates also lowers the risk of
loss, damage or theft.

Other important factors to consider when selecting
materials to digitise are the uniqueness of the materials,
their potential value to users, and the degree to which they
support the mission of the institution as stated in its
digitisation policy. Questions to ask include:

- *Are the materials unique or rare?* Digitising materials –
  manuscripts, photographs, letters, diaries, rare books –
  that are found nowhere else benefits users that might
  otherwise have no way of accessing valuable items. The
  great promise of the global digital library is the
  accessibility of primary sources to scholars everywhere,
  reducing the need for expensive travel to faraway archives.
  For the first time, items once restricted in access only to
  credentialed researchers are available to the general public.
  For example, school children can now view the Magna
  Carta on the British Library's website. There is an ethical
  obligation for institutions to support the vision of the
  global digital library by making the unique items they
  hold as widely available as possible. Digitisation of unique
  materials is an ethical use of the limited resources available
  for digital projects for another reason: there is no danger
  of duplicating the efforts of another institution.

- *Do the items have cultural or historical significance?*
  Materials with cultural or historical significance, especially
  those of importance to the region in which the holding
  institution is located, should be given priority. Digitisation
  can play an important role in enhancing access to

resources that can be of enormous benefit to scholars and to the general public. A number of the digital collections at Oklahoma State University (OSU) relate to American Indians, because they play a significant role in the history and culture of Oklahoma. The state was once known as Indian Territory and was designated as land for the native tribes who had been displaced by white settlement.[1] The name 'Oklahoma' is taken from an Indian word meaning 'red earth'. Oklahoma has a significant Indian population and is the location of the headquarters of 34 tribes, so it was natural for the OSU Library to focus a number of its digitisation project on materials for or about American Indians. The first digital project undertaken by the OSU Library was the digitisation of Charles Kappler's *Indian Affairs: Laws and Treaties*, a collection of all US laws and treaties pertaining to the federally recognised tribes published by the US Government Printing Office (GPO). The work is unique in that (1) it brings all laws and treaties pertinent to the practice of Indian law conveniently together in one place and (2) it has valuable annotations added by the editor, Mr Kappler, that provide useful citations, cross-references and legislative history. The annotations also function as a browsing tool facilitating the location of the researcher's subject of interest by summarising the issues dealt with in particular sections of the treaty or law. Despite its usefulness to tribes, courts and Indian law attorneys, *Kappler* (as it is commonly called) has been out of print for some time and is not available in any of the commercial legal databases. It can also be difficult to find a set of the books in libraries: there are only five complete sets in the state of Oklahoma, which has two large federal depository libraries that receive copies of all materials published by the GPO, and two law schools, the University of Oklahoma and the University of Tulsa, that offer advanced degrees in Indian law. Of these five sets, the majority are in deteriorating condition due to age and heavy use. The lack of access to such an important tool was a problem throughout 'Indian Country', those portions of the western USA and Alaska where most American Indians live today and where the vast majority of tribes are headquartered. Because it was originally published before 1923 and because it is a US government publication, there were no copyright restrictions on *Kappler*. For these reasons, the OSU Library decided it was a very appropriate choice for the first electronic publication by OSU. The OSU Electronic Publishing Center (EPC) has since published online the *Decisions of the Indian Claims Commission*, a collection of legal cases interpreting the rights of tribes under the treaties. The EPC is beginning a project to digitise the letters of David Pendleton Oakerhater, the first American Indian saint and is also planning a project that will record and document endangered Indian languages.

- *Are the materials in high demand?* If so, digitisation would provide a benefit to both the patrons who want to use the materials, and to the staff who handle patron requests. One of our most popular and useful projects at Oklahoma State University has been the digitisation of annual course catalogues from 1980 to present. These catalogues contain descriptions of courses offered at the university, and are frequently requested by alumni who are applying to graduate school and who need to demonstrate that a course they took at OSU meets the requirements for prerequisites set by the institution to which they are applying. Staff in the registrar's office and in university archives spent hours every week searching old catalogues for course descriptions and making copies to send to the requesting alumni. By digitising the catalogues and making them available on the university website, the OSU Library saved staff time and resources and also provided a simple way for alumni to immediately get the course descriptions they needed from the convenience of their desktops. This is a project that, while it did not digitally preserve rare and fragile materials or make a great historical treasure available online, truly did provide a great good for a great number of people. It had the added benefit of generating goodwill toward the Library and the EPC among the university administration and among alumni, something that could lead to support from these important constituencies for future digitisation projects.

- *How will enhancing access to these materials serve users and meet the goals of the institution?* To answer this question, you will need to know who your users are. There will be the primary audience, the constituency your institution exists to serve, and the secondary audience, those who use and benefit from your website although it is not planned for or paid for by them. For universities, primary users are the faculty, students, researchers and staff. Important secondary users are alumni and, particularly for state-funded institutions, the residents of the state or region where the institution is located. National libraries and archives serve the people of their nation in general, though often their efforts are primarily concentrated on the needs of government officials and departments. Whoever the primary audience may be, the digital library constructed to serve it should select items for digitisation that will be of major interest and usefulness to that population. Consult the collection policies for the 'brick and mortar' library of the institution, as well as your written digitisation policy if you have one, to determine the subject areas in which the institution collects heavily. Surveys of the user population to determine areas of interest, and studies of usage statistics for the print and analogue collections as well as existing digital collections can provide useful data for selection decisions.

■ *Will digitisation increase functionality as well as access?* Some items may be more useful in a digital format that will permit searching or manipulation. This is especially true for print works that are indexed poorly or not at all. One of the reasons the OSU Library decided, in collaboration with the University of Tulsa Mabee Legal Information Center, to digitise the *Decisions of the Indian Claims Commission* was the fact that volumes 30 through 43, containing many of the final decisions and awards, had not been indexed, making it very difficult to locate particular cases. We began the digital project with these volumes, and will continue digitising earlier volumes as funds become available.

Digitisation can also improve the functionality of maps and images by allowing users to zoom in on a particular area to see greater detail. Of course, digitisation can also increase the risk of images being stolen, manipulated or misused. Users must be able to trust that the electronic files in our digital libraries are accurate and authentic, and digital librarians have an ethical obligation to protect the integrity of digital collections to the extent that this is possible. It is far easier to change a digital version of a document without detection than to alter a print version unobtrusively. Computer security is not only good policy but an ethical obligation. That said, no security system is perfect – such security does not exist – so we must not assure donors, grant making agencies or users that our site is hack-proof. Still, we must protect our servers to the best of our ability, back up our files, and implement practices to discourage image theft, such as use of lower resolution images. Requiring free registration may help deter those who would misuse the contents of your digital collection. Include a terms of use statement and copyright notices on your website where appropriate, as some users may otherwise misuse digital materials with no intention of doing harm. What a user may or may not do with the contents of an online collection must be made very clear in order to prevent unintentional misuse. An online statement of terms of use will not discourage the true thief, who does not care about the legality of what they are doing, but it will strengthen the institution's case against anyone who appropriates or misuses the digital materials as it removes the argument that the transgressor didn't know what they were doing was forbidden or illegal.

■ *Will this project generate positive publicity that could attract future funding or collaborators?* This question may sound calculating and mercenary, but it can be a legitimate factor in making sound selection decisions. The materials in question might not be your institution's first choice for digitisation, but if they do have merit and will allow you to establish a relationship with a partner institution, a benefactor or a funding entity, the greater good will be served by proceeding with the project in order to build a relationship. In several instances, the EPC has assisted OSU faculty or departments with digitisation projects in order to build support for the

Library and the EPC. We have done pro bono work on other projects with the hope that we will later be able to obtain funding to digitise additional materials.

One effective method for evaluating digital projects under consideration is the decision matrix, which can be useful in quantifying the merits of various projects and performing the ethical function of reducing bias in the deliberation process. A decision matrix sets forth questions based on the selection criteria you have established that must be answered yes or no. Your answers to these questions guide you through assessing the project to determine whether it should be undertaken. An excellent guide for establishing a selection decision matrix is set forth in Chapter 2 of Stuart D. Lee's *Digital Imaging: A Practical Handbook* (2001). A version of Lee's decision matrix is also available online as an appendix to 'Scoping the Future of the University of Oxford's Digital Library Collections' (*http://www.bodley.ox.ac.uk/scoping/report.html*).

Copyright: the 800 pound (or kilo) gorilla

One of the first questions that should be asked in your selection matrix is, 'Is the material under copyright?' Many times an affirmative answer to this question brings the prospective project to a screeching halt. Though librarians and open access advocates can see it as a stumbling block, copyright plays an essential role in the advancement of knowledge, arts and sciences by providing creators of materials with limited exclusive rights as an economic incentive. All codes of conduct for information professionals stress the importance of respecting copyright and intellectual property rights, and legal penalties for violating copyright can be harsh to the point of draconian. Therefore, one of the greatest ethical obligations in selection is determining the rights status of a work under consideration for digitisation, both from the aspect of respecting the rights of the creator or owner of the work (not necessarily the same entity) and of protecting your institution from the legal ramifications of copyright violation.

It can be very difficult to determine the copyright status of a work depending on if it was published, when it was published, where it was published, and if copyright has been renewed. The laws in this area are complicated and vary from country to country, so it is always wise to consult legal counsel when there is any doubt. In the USA, one is generally safe with old (pre-1923) published materials and with materials produced by federal government agencies, which are automatically in the public domain, no matter when they were produced. Peter Hirtle of Cornell University has developed a chart, 'Copyright Term and the Public Domain in the United States', that is helpful in determining the copyright status of both published and unpublished works (Hirtle, 2006). The Cornell University Library Copyright Center (*http://www.copyright.cornell.edu*), contains links to laws, FAQs, tutorials and permission forms. Another helpful online resource, particularly for US copyright law, is the Collaborative Digitization Program's 'Legal, Copyright & Intellectual Property Resources' (*http://www.cdpheritage.org/digital/legal.cfm*), with links to the aforementioned chart, and to an excellent guide to intellectual property questions that must be answered before undertaking a digitisation project, 'Legal Issues to Consider When Digitising Collections' (Helig, 2004). This helpful document covers published and unpublished works, images and photographs, and special cases like letters and diaries donated to libraries or archives.

The University of Texas provides an online crash course in copyright law (Harper, 2001) and an online tutorial complete with quiz (*http://www.lib.utsystem.edu/copyright/*). For international copyright laws, consult the World Intellectual Property Organization website (*http://www.wipo.int/copyright/en/index.html*). Help with UK intellectual property laws may be found on the government-sponsored site (*http://www.intellectual-property.gov.uk/std/resources/copyright/index.htm*) and on the Chartered Institute of Library and Information Professionals (CILIP) and Library Association Copyright Alliance (LACA) website (*http://www.cilip.org.uk/professionalguidance/copyright/advice*). As information professionals, we are bound by our codes of professional conduct to respect intellectual property and we have an ethical duty to educate ourselves as much as possible about the issue to avoid any inadvertent violation of copyright law and an ethical duty to consult legal counsel when in doubt about the public domain or ownership status of any item.

Handling privacy issues

Librarians are used to protecting the privacy of their patrons; this principle is stressed in every library association's code of professional ethics. A basic tenet of librarianship, open access to information, can come into direct conflict with another ethical issue: protecting the privacy of those whose private papers are made available to the public, and the privacy of the third parties mentioned or addressed in these documents. Among information professionals, only archivists are accustomed to dealing with this issue, and the Society of American Archivists' Code of Ethics addresses this dilemma in Section VII, Privacy and Restricted Information:

> Archivists respect the privacy of individuals who created, or are the subjects of, documentary materials of long-term value, especially those who had no voice in the disposition of the materials.

The commentary on this section advises archivists to 'weigh the need for openness and the need to respect privacy rights to determine whether the release of records or information would constitute an invasion of privacy'. It is a delicate balancing act, and one which librarians, with their passion for access to information, may find especially difficult.

These privacy concerns do not generally arise in published works – any disputes over the content have no doubt been settled through legal channels long before the book reaches a library. In the case of personal papers donated or sold to an archive, library or museum, no such vetting has taken place, and it falls to the archivist/librarian/curator to review the materials and identify any possible problems. The first question to be answered is whether or not the persons mentioned in the documents are still alive. The archivist for the United Methodist Church of the United States consulted historians, theologians, and fellow archivists for guidance in making letters written by missionaries available to researchers. The criterion adopted for non-disclosure of records was whether 'the information released 'might cause personal harm or deep embarrassment' to a living person' (Schwartz, 2005). A 50-year restriction on letters and a 75-year restriction on 'confidential and personal papers' were determined to be the best ways to protect the privacy of the living. This decision was made with regard to merely opening the archived materials to onsite researchers. Putting personal papers online makes them much more widely available and increases the risks to privacy.

If you are dealing with materials over 100 years old – letters from the American Civil War, for example – you can be reasonably confident that the writers, correspondents and subjects of the letters, and their immediate families, are no longer alive and that it is safe to proceed with digitisation. When dealing with the documents of a still living or recently deceased person, the situation is more complicated. In determining whether the institution even has the right to digitise the materials, it will be necessary to check the deed of gift to see if all rights of copyright were assigned to the library. If not, the donor or the donor's heirs must be contacted before the library can proceed with a digitisation project. New deeds of gift or purchase agreements should specify whether digitisation of items in the collection is permitted, and if there are to be any time restrictions before they can be put online. In 'Legal Issues to Consider When Digitising Collections', Jean Helig (2004) advises contacting addressees as well as authors of letters before proceeding with digitisation, even if intellectual property rights have been assigned to the archive. Helig also urges consultation with legal counsel about any sensitive information contained in the documents. Archivists and librarians, when negotiating the acquisition of papers, must balance the public's right of access to materials against the privacy rights of the individuals who may be mentioned in those papers. These persons should be consulted before their private letters are made available to the world. Time restrictions such as those imposed in the United Methodist Church case are a workable solution for protecting the privacy and feelings of individuals and their families. Although professional codes of conduct for archivists direct members to discourage restrictions and to agree only to strictly limited restrictions on access, they also recognise an ethical obligation to protect innocent third parties. The greater good is served by open access to knowledge, but not at the expense of 'personal harm or deep embarrassment to a living person' (Schwartz, 2005). In *Without Consent: The Ethics of Disclosing Personal Information in Public Archives*, Heather MacNeil (1992) observes:

> [A]ny ethical stance constrains someone's freedom; that does not mean such a stance is unreasonable or unjust. In the end, our acceptance of limitations on the pursuit of knowledge in order to protect a greater common interest is what distinguishes us as moral beings.

Note

1. Tribal members prefer the term 'American Indian' to 'Native American'.

5

Ethics and funding

Every institution must find a way to fund its digital library. Eventually, digital projects will likely be considered such an essential library service that they will be included in the library's budget, as are subscriptions to databases, rather than requiring outside funding. In the meantime, digital librarians will need to spend a good portion of their time seeking funding from government agencies, private foundations, corporate sponsors or individual donors. This chapter examines the ethical considerations related to these funding opportunities.

Grants

Grants are the lifeblood of most digital projects, and many of these grants come from government agencies or government-funded agencies. In the USA, major sources of government funding include the National Endowment for the Humanities and Institute for Museum and Library Services. In the UK, The Joint Information Systems Committee is the main source of government grants, while throughout the European Union funding for digital projects comes from the eContent*plus* programme. The Australian Research Council is the primary funding agency for digitisation Down Under. Private philanthropic organisations such as the Mellon

Foundation or Carnegie Corporation of New York also are giving grants for digitisation. Whether dealing with a government agency or private foundation, the ethical considerations are much the same. First, be sure that your project really matches the programme description or solicitation for proposals issued by the funder. It wastes your time and theirs to try to make a project fit into a grant programme that is really intended for other purposes. If you aren't sure whether a particular grant opportunity is appropriate for your project, contact the programme officer. Describe your project to the programme officer in an e-mail and enquire whether their organisation is interested in funding such a project under this grant programme. Sometimes part of your project will be eligible while another part will not. You can then concentrate your efforts on writing a proposal for funding the eligible portion and find other funding for the remaining part. When dealing with funding agencies, as with any other party, it is ethical as well as simply polite not to waste their time. Submitting an inappropriate grant proposal to a grant-maker is like Cinderella's stepsisters mutilating their oversized feet to fit the glass slipper; it won't work and it only hurts you. The funding community is relatively small, and funders communicate with one another. You don't want to develop a reputation for interpreting the grant programme guidelines 'creatively' to suit your own purposes.

Be honest, accurate and realistic in your grant proposals. Obviously, you should not lie, exaggerate, obfuscate or mislead the grant-maker about any aspect of your project or its goals, objectives, methods, timetable, participants or their qualifications. I emphasise accuracy because there can be a temptation even among the scrupulously honest to overestimate what we can reasonably accomplish in the given time and with the given amount of money. Look hard at the tasks, the schedule and the budget for your project, and ask yourself, your colleagues and perhaps an outside expert if what you are planning is realistic. Use previous projects to help make that determination. If you have no experience in this area, contact someone at another institution with experience in digital projects and ask their advice. One of the first things a grant reviewer does is look at the budget and at the timetable to determine if the project is feasible. Many proposals don't pass this initial test, so it is not only ethical but in the best interest of your institution to be as accurate and realistic as possible. Budgets are a particular concern, because it can be just as bad to receive more money than you need as it is to receive less than enough. This seems strange, because in our personal budgets and in planning the annual departmental budget, ending up with more money than we need is not usually seen as problem. Rather, we are congratulated on our money management skills if we bring a project in under budget. However, for grant-makers this can cause a huge problem. In the USA, private foundations are required by the tax code to give away a certain percentage of their funds every year. If your project comes in under budget and you have to return money to the funding foundation, they will have difficulties with the tax authorities because you have, in essence, prevented them from giving away the required quota of funds. Similarly, if government agencies do not expend all the funds they have encumbered for projects during their fiscal year, they are at risk of having their own funding cut for the following year by the legislative budget process. Consequently, it is incumbent upon us to be as precise as possible in our budgeting, both to protect our institutions from the problems caused by a shortfall and to protect our funders from the problems caused by overages.

When applying for grants, we have ethical duties to our institutions, to the grant-makers, and to other grant seekers.

It is important to follow grant guidelines religiously, down to width of margins, size and style of font and placement of page. Proposals that fail to comply with these seemingly trivial requirements are usually screened out on these grounds before they are even read. The most worthy project can be declined for failure to use the proper font. What may seem like capricious behaviour on the part of funding bodies is usually a response to past abuses by applicants trying to get around page limits. This is an excellent example of why we have an ethical duty to follow grant guidelines exactly to avoid penalising our institutions and fellow or future grant applicants. Make sure to acknowledge any grant support on the website of the funded project. This is not only ethical but, as your mother would point out, just good manners.

Resist the temptation to file grant requests for the same project with multiple funding agencies. Should more than one be funded, you will have more money than you need for your project and you will have caused serious problems for the grant-makers and for the other grant applicants whose proposals were declined in favour of yours. When seeking funds from more than one source, the ethical thing to do is to make all funders aware of the other grant-makers you are approaching and the amount you have requested from them. If your needs exceed the amount of money the funding sources can award, it is best to go to them in advance and ask what percentage of your project they might be able to fund. Apply to them for that amount and seek the remainder of the funds elsewhere. True, you may not get all the funds you need from the various grant-makers on the first attempt, but you have behaved ethically and dealt honestly with the funders. During the next round of applications, funders will remember you as an honest broker. A good reputation is priceless.

Grant-makers have ethical obligations as well. First and foremost, they must be fair and unbiased, avoiding favouritism and political cronyism. Some grant funding agencies tend to support the same applicants over and over again, rarely taking on projects from unfamiliar applicants. There is a rationale for this decision: they know that funds given to a proven success will not be wasted or misused. It does, however, make it difficult for new players, especially those from smaller institutions, to get in the game. Most organisations that fund digitisation projects focus on encouraging technological innovation, which has been a great boon to the development of digital libraries. However, this focus on technology can sometimes be taken to such an extreme that they fund projects that are exciting but are unsustainable as long-term digital assets. If an agency pours large amounts of finite funds – especially public funds – into a project, they have an ethical obligation to ensure that the digital objects produced will stand the test of time and will not become unusable in five years. Funding agencies should also be aware of the burden some of their requirements may put on grant applicants. Demanding expensive binders and dozens of copies can run up costs for applicants, sometimes to the point of making the grant proposal too expensive to submit. Electronic applications remove the need for such trappings and are more equitable for all applicants.

As digital librarians, you may be asked by a funding organisation to act as a peer reviewer of grant proposals. In this capacity you will have the opportunity to exercise the ethics you always hope the grant-maker will have when you are an applicant. Be aware of personal biases and make an effort to restrain their influence. Resist any tendency or pressure to engage in favouritism, politics or cronyism. Try not to be dazzled by presentation and to focus on content. Finally, keep an open mind about unfamiliar applicants and make an impartial judgment based on the merits of the project.

Corporate sponsorship

There will rarely be an ethical dilemma concerning whether or not to apply for a grant. This is not true when it comes to corporate sponsorship. Some corporations that commit transgressions against the environment or the workforce, for example, may try to buy goodwill by making philanthropic donations. When seeking or accepting corporate sponsorships, we must first ask ourselves whether this is a company with which we want to be associated. Some may argue that money is money, and ask 'Why not take funds from wealthy corporations, whatever their reputation?' However, we must be aware of the impact a certain corporate logo might have on the credibility of our website. Rarely do corporations give something for nothing, and at the very least they will likely want their name and/or corporate logo displayed on the website they sponsor. When researchers see that your digital library receives support from a corporate sponsor – especially one with a reputation for dubious ethics – they may wonder what influence or control this sponsor has over the contents of your site. One way people judge us is by the company we keep, and the wrong association can damage your professional reputation and credibility. I have seen museum exhibits underwritten by corporate sponsors so improbable or preposterous that I actually thought it was a joke perpetrated by a mischievous intern. You do not want researchers to have a similar reaction when they pull up your website. If a company's values do not reflect or support those of your institution, they will probably not be an appropriate corporate sponsor. If a company seeks to impose editorial control or to censor what you publish online, then that company is not an appropriate sponsor. Such restrictions on academic freedom of expression can never be ethical or acceptable. There are many fine companies who support digital projects and who make no attempt to control the content of the websites. Much of the infrastructure required to start major digitisation programmes in the USA was acquired through the generosity of technology companies that made monetary or in-kind donations to digital projects. As government funding for the arts and humanities continues to decline, we may be forced to rely more and more on the private sector for support.

Individual donors

The concerns and considerations about individual donors are similar to those for corporate sponsors. Once again, our first concern is with the reputation of the donor: is this someone with whom our institution wishes to be associated? Will this association enhance or harm our own reputation and credibility? Wealthy individuals, like wealthy corporations, may attempt to buy respectability or to atone for past sins by associating themselves with a worthy cause or institution. We must ask ourselves to what extent our own reputation and integrity are for sale, and also how self-righteous we can afford to be. Funds are scarce, period, and we may not always be able to refuse funds from a source we would prefer to avoid. It is essential that we never compromise our editorial control over the contents of our online exhibits and publications; that would be the ultimate betrayal of our users and the height of unethical behaviour for any information professional. All of our codes of ethics are steadfast on the issue of intellectual freedom, and we must never forget this ethical obligation.

Another problem that may arise with individual donors is the wish of a wealthy supporter or alumnus to use your digital library as a venue for his or her own 'vanity' publication: the novel, memoir or diary they are sure the world wants to see. This situation is a delicate one requiring great tact. While it would not be ethical to dilute your collections with an unworthy publication, neither would it be smart to alienate a generous supporter. Perhaps you can arrive at some compromise, such as digitising the work and making CDs of it for the donor to present to his or her friends and associates. Consult your archivists or special collections librarians for a tactful way to handle the situation; they often have experience with accepting collections they do not want or need from people they do not wish to offend. Often one can fall back on the collection (or digitisation) policy, citing the specifications set forth therein for materials to be published. This is yet another reason to have such a policy in place.

Sustaining digital collections

An ongoing problem is funding the maintenance of our digital collections. Typically, grant funds or donations are available for funding digitisation projects, but not for preservation. Institutions have to find a way to cover the ongoing costs, and digital librarians have an ethical duty to raise this issue with their administrations. If they are to survive, digital libraries must become a regular part of a library's infrastructure, just as much as bricks and mortar and books. If there is no institutional commitment to the ongoing preservation and maintenance of digital collections, then it is a waste of precious resources to undertake the digitisation of materials in the first place. Digitisation centres could certainly benefit from an endowment fund that would provide continuing support over the years. Consider working with your library's development officer or your institution's fundraising arm to explore the possibility of creating such an endowment. Such arrangements have been used over the years to sustain buildings and special collections; digital collections seem a natural fit for this funding tool. An endowment fund would allow the institution to seek donations of all sizes from many donors, eliminating the control a single sponsor might seek to have over the operation. We have a duty to our collections, our users and our institutions to explore creative and ethical sources of ongoing funds for our digital libraries.

6

Ethics and digital collaborations

Collaboration is essential to building digital libraries. Many digital projects involve at least one other partner. Collaborative efforts have many advantages: ideally, partners bring different yet complementary skills and assets to the project, making it possible to create a bigger and better collection than could be digitised by one institution alone. Funding agencies look favourably on collaborations, because they feel their money is benefiting more parties. When choosing a partner for a digital project, as when choosing a partner in business or in life, it is most important to find one whose ethics and values are compatible with your own. Successful collaboration requires mutual respect and trust (Schrage, 1995; NINCH, 2002), which in turn depend on shared ethics.

Evaluating prospective partners

Before entering into a collaboration, you should thoroughly investigate prospective partners, both the institutions involved and the individuals at the institutions with whom you will be working. There are a number of ways to collect information that will aid you in making a decision:

■ Read the mission and/or vision statements of the institutions and the departments (e.g. library, digitisation centre, archive) that would be involved in the project. The lack of such a statement can also give you valuable information: they may not have thought out what they want to do, who or what they want to be, and how they plan to arrive at these goals.

- Look at any previous digital projects potential collaborators have undertaken. Do these projects comply with the kinds of requirements you set for your own projects, in terms of standard file formats, platform-independent software, and accessibility? If there were other institutions involved with those projects, contact them and ask how the project went and whether they would work again with the institution in question and the individuals involved.

- Use a search engine such as Google to research the organisation and the individuals involved. You never know what you might find.

- Look at the curricula vitae or web pages of the individuals who would be working on the project with you. Do they belong to any professional organisations? Are they active members (e.g. officers, committees)? Look at the code of ethics for these professional organisations – is it similar to the professional conduct codes to which you adhere?

- Research whether the individuals have been involved in any sort of collaborative activity: research project, article or book, conference panel or presentation. Contact the colleagues with whom they worked to find out more about their working style.

- Consider whether you and the individuals in question have colleagues or acquaintances in common. In the rather small world of libraries, archives and digitisation centres, it is likely you have mutual acquaintances who can provide insight on whether you would work well together. One of my best partnerships, which has extended to a number of projects, resulted from an introduction by a colleague who knew us both and thought that given our similar interests and personalities, we might make a good team.

■ Talk to your prospective partners and be honest with them about your own working style and expectations. If you have to have things done two weeks before they're due and your partner works right up until midnight on the deadline to get the job done, you're probably going to drive each other crazy. You don't have to have exactly the same approach to work; complementary styles can make stronger teams. It's good to have at least one person who sees the big picture and one who concentrates on details. Big-picture types will never get the little things done, while detail-oriented types can get so caught up in minutia that they lose sight of their overall goals.

■ Consider doing a small pilot project with your prospective partner first, as a limited commitment will allow you to see how well you work together.

Proceeding with a collaboration

The best way to begin a collaboration is with a written agreement that sets forth each party's rights and responsibilities, the schedule and duration of the project, the handling of funds from whatever source, and the procedure to be followed if a party needs to withdraw from the project before it is completed. Putting everything into a written agreement clarifies what is to be done, who is going to do what task, and how the project, including funds, will be managed. Putting everything into writing eliminates confusion and gives you a source to turn to for guidance if disagreements arise. It can be an informal document, but it should be signed by administrators from all institutions involved, documenting the commitment of each organisation's management to the project. There should also be a brief mission statement for the project, setting forth its goals, objectives and values. I realise that I advocate a lot of written documentation – collections policies, mission statements, collaboration agreements – but writing things down is the best way to ensure that everyone understands the purpose of an endeavour and their place in it. Written agreements force us to think about our motives, our goals and our ethics, and they provide both guidance and protection. Writing all these things may seem like a waste of time, but it will save time in the long run, helping you to avoid disagreements and helping to resolve those that do arise. None of these documents need be an elaborate legal document; a simple statement of purpose, and a delineation of what is to be done, when it is to be done, and who is responsible for doing it will suffice.

When working with others, we obviously have an ethical duty to deal fairly with them. Invoking the 'golden rule' and treating them as we wish to be treated is an excellent guide. Every human relationship requires a good deal of compromise, understanding, forgiveness and kindness. Communication is always a key to success. When working on projects we owe our partners a duty to keep them informed, and they owe the same duty to us. We must also make a concerted effort to understand the organisational culture of our partner institutions and the expectations and constraints that go along with it. Libraries, museums and archives have very different organisational cultures, and non-profit or academic environments differ considerably from corporations. Try to explain your culture to your partners and make an effort to understand theirs. Something you might initially consider an affront may simply be a difference in corporate cultures. Naturally, you will find some people easier to work with than others, but whatever your personal feelings about the people you may have to deal with on a joint project, you must put the good of your institution first and not allow your own dislike of or difficulties with partners to stand in the way of accomplishing the project's goals. Of course, you should never betray your ethical principles to keep a project on track.

Sometimes, no matter how carefully you have vetted your partners, you may find that you are involved with someone whose ethics, whether personal or institutional, you cannot abide. There are issues on which there can be no ethical compromise. Those unique to digital projects include the use of standard file formats and platform-independent, non-proprietary software, accessibility issues and observance of copyright restrictions. Disagreement on any of the above can lead to the dissolution of a collaborative effort. I have recommended my own institution withdraw from a joint project when I became concerned over other participants' resistance to adhering to best practice standards and their insistence on using a custom designed, proprietary software. There were also disagreements on commercialisation of the site, and whether it would be appropriate to charge for hard copies of images. Administrators at my university library felt that any commercialisation of the site would damage its credibility with the scholars and serious researchers who were one of its main audiences. Consequently, we decided to withdraw from the project rather than compromise our strongly held beliefs on these issues. For us, it was a question of ethics.

Ending a collaboration

When you must withdraw from a collaboration, be honest with your partner(s) about why you are leaving and do what you can to minimise the damage caused by your decision. The other institutions have a right to know why you want to pull out of the project, and it may be that discovering how strongly you feel about an issue will be enough to get them to change their position. However, it would definitely be unethical to threaten to withdraw in an attempt to force such a change of heart. If neither side is willing to compromise and you must leave the project, follow the exit strategy set forth in your written partnership agreement. If you don't have such an agreement, use common sense and common courtesy to get out of the situation. Do give the others some notice, if at all possible. If you are working with a number of partners, and your disagreement is primarily with one of the institutions, do not try to influence the other participants to join you in leaving the project. They must make their own decisions based on their own ethical standards. Do not engage in acrimonious exchanges or resort to *ad hominem* attacks. While you must stand up for your ethical standards, it is not necessary or desirable to do so in a very public and self-righteous way. A sanctimonious approach may alienate your former partners and possible future partners.

Like any other break-up, this situation should be handled discreetly. Explain your reasons to your partners and your backers, if any, but do not gossip about the situation with other colleagues. If asked why your institution withdrew from a project, you can simply say 'We decided to go in a different direction' or cite the ever-popular 'creative differences'. If someone who is considering working with your former partner contacts you for a reference, be honest without vilifying the institution or any individual. You can explain differences in organisational culture that underlay your problems or the differences in your views on certain issues without being unfair or unethical to either the party asking the questions or the party they are investigating. You should also be honest if you are asked if you would work with the other party again – if the positions were reversed, you would want the other person to be honest with you on this score.

Division of property is another problem that arises in most separations. When the partnership breaks apart it is likely there will be some disagreement over who owns what, whether the items in question are the digital files – digitised text or images – whose creation was the impetus for the project, or other intangibles, such as designs, ideas or titles. The best way to avoid such a situation is to cover ownership questions in the initial partnership agreement. If one of your partners pulls out of a project, for whatever reason, the most ethical thing to do is to return to them the things they brought to the table, such as graphics or web designs created by their employees, and to remove from the project website anything – logos or insignia, for example – that would suggest the institution is still involved in the project. If you are the one leaving the project, request in writing that your institution's name and logo be removed from all project websites and communications, and ask that any copies of digital files you consider to be the property of your institution be deleted from the computers of other project members. Should you discover that your former partners are still using your materials, consult with your dean or administrator for the best way to handle the situation. Often a telephone call or e-mail from an administration official at your institution to an administration official at the former partner institution will solve the problem informally and quietly. If at all possible, you want to avoid involving legal counsel and getting into an ugly confrontation that will reflect poorly on both institutions.

Conclusion

Collaboration can be both a great opportunity and a great risk. Most of us will need to work with others to accomplish some of our projects, and collaborations make it possible to do more than a single institution could ever accomplish on its own. By collaborating, we can share resources, reunite dispersed collections, improve access to and awareness of rare materials, and increase our chances of receiving grant funds. Unfortunately, we can also sometimes find ourselves in untenable situations with partners whose ethics and outlooks do not match our own. A collaboration should not be entered into lightly, but rather cautiously and thoughtfully. A few basic rules to observe:

- *Rule 1:* Know your prospective partner:
  - What is their mission?
  - What are their goals?
  - What is their motivation for getting into this partnership?
  - What is their organisational culture, and what are the differences between it and that of your institution?
  - To what codes of professional ethics do they subscribe?
  - What do their past partners have to say about them?

- *Rule 2:* Get it in writing. To avoid confusion and conflict later, you will need a written agreement that does the following:
  - States the mission and goals of the project.
  - Outlines each party's rights and responsibilities.
  - Sets forth the ownership rights of each party as to the digital objects created for the project and to incidental digital files or designs that may remain the property of the creating institution.
  - Contains an equitable exit strategy in the event a party needs to withdraw before the project is completed.

- *Rule 3:* Treat your partners with the same respect and courtesy you would want to receive from them:
  - Different institutions (libraries, museum, archives) have different organisational cultures; try to understand and respect those of your colleagues.
  - Know what the codes of ethics for your partners' professions require, and explain to them what your code of conduct requires. Where differences exist, discuss ways to handle them.

- *Rule 4:* Communicate, communicate, communicate:
  - It is essential to communicate openly and honestly with *all* of your partners. Nothing is more disastrous to a collaboration than for cliques to form among the partners.
  - Be open and honest about your concerns, your expectations and your activities. Secrecy will most likely be viewed as deception.

- *Rule 5:* If you feel you would violate the ethical principles of your profession or your institution by continuing to participate in the project, withdraw:

- Try to minimise damage to the project that will result from your withdrawal.
- Be frank with your partners about your reasons for withdrawing.
- Be discreet with outsiders about your reasons for withdrawing.

7

Ethics and digitisation standards

The use of established standards is one of the greatest ethical obligations of digital librarians. Why are standards so important? Because the usefulness, accessibility and durability of our digital libraries depends upon them. Librarians have a long history of working with standards; we have long recognised their critical role in finding information. Classification systems and controlled vocabularies are among the powerful tools based on agreed-upon standards. Standards have the same significance in the online world:

- Standard file formats minimise our dependence on operating systems, proprietary software and particular types of hardware.

- Standards facilitate interoperability with other digital libraries, and maximise the accessibility of digital collections.

- Standards increase the likelihood that our collections will remain operational over the long term.

- We owe it to our users, our institutions and our funders to make the best possible use of resources to create digital collections built to last, and to be accessible and usable by the widest possible audience.

■ Our professional codes of conduct require the highest level of service possible within available resources. Standards help us to fulfil this duty.

Standards are essential in two areas of digital libraries: file formats and metadata. The International Organization for Standardization (ISO) is the ultimate authority for many technical standards. ISO, a non-governmental organisation, is the largest developer of standards in the world. It is comprised of a network of the national standards organisations for 156 countries (as of December 2005). ISO was founded in 1946 'to facilitate the international coordination and unification of industrial standards' (ISO, 2005). These national standards organisations propose standards, and delegates from member nations work with experts at the ISO Central Secretariat to develop those standards that will be adopted and published by ISO. The ISO standards are voluntary, but the need for standards in developing global businesses has made their adoption advantageous for nations, businesses and academia. The most important ISO standards for digital libraries are ISO 19005, the standard for PDF files; Standard Generalised Markup Language, ISO 8879, the mother of all mark-up languages, including HTML and XML; and ISO 646, commonly referred to as ASCII, for text files. The major file standards for images are JPEG2000, a standard developed by the Joint Photographic Experts Group (a working group formed by ISO and the International Telecommunications Union), and TIFF (Tagged Image File Format), an open proprietary file specification controlled by Adobe Systems that has become the de facto standard for uncompressed image files.

Other standards important to digital libraries are the XML Document Type Definitions (DTD) and XML Schema for the Text Encoding Initiative (TEI), Encoded Archival Description (EAD), Dublin Core, and Metadata Encoding and Transmission Standard (METS). These standards may be agreed upon by a community of interest (TEI was developed by academics digitising texts for linguistic analysis; EAD was developed by archivists for their finding aids) or by a national standards organisation (METS is a Library of Congress standard). Regardless of where they were developed, file format standards allow for accessibility by any platform, require no or free software (Adobe Reader, browser), make files more portable, and promote the long-term preservation of files. Some organisations, like the World Wide Web Consortium (W3C) release 'recommendations' rather than standards because they are not official standard-making bodies. These recommendations, such as those of the W3C on Web accessibility, carry the weight of standards for those working on websites, and what is said in this chapter regarding standards also applies to them.

Metadata standards have long been used by the library community in our systems of cataloguing, classification and controlled vocabulary. Librarians invented metadata, and our standardised systems of organising information about information are probably the best known fact about the profession. Librarian jokes, for example, almost always reference the Dewey Decimal System in addition to cardigans and glasses. They are an important part of the librarian stereotype and one that even those of us who wouldn't be caught dead in sensible shoes can be proud of. MARC records revolutionised the ability to search the contents of libraries around the world. A researcher can use the WorldCat database to search the catalogues of libraries on every continent for a specific item. In MARC records, numbered fields are assigned to the various items of information that can be used as access points to find materials. The MARC standard originated with the US Library of Congress, but has been implemented by libraries around the world. A newer effort to establish an international standard for metadata is the Dublin Core, named after the Dublin, Ohio headquarters of the Online Computer Library Center (OCLC) where the initial meetings were held. Dublin Core is more flexible than the MARC format, and can be adapted for many formats and for use by non-library organisations such as museums. It requires less training than cataloguing in MARC records because the element names (e.g. title, creator, format) are simpler and more self-explanatory than the elaborate numbering system used for MARC fields. The Dublin Core Metadata Element Set Version 1.1 specifying the 15 required elements for Dublin Core records became an ISO standard (15836) in 2003 (Dublin Core Metadata Initiative, 2003). Dublin Core records are ideally suited for digital libraries, and indeed one of the driving forces in the development of the Dublin Core was the need to catalogue digital materials. Wide implementation of Dublin Core is central to the development of a worldwide catalogue of digital resources, such as that envisioned by the open access movement. Other digital library standards, such as TEI, EAD and TIFF, have their own metadata embedded in headers within the files, but Dublin Core records can easily be created from this information. Adobe Acrobat software allows creators to add metadata to PDF files and this is a convenient place to insert the Dublin Core metadata elements for that resource. Additionally, digital repository software like DSpace, Greenstone, E-prints or Digital Commons allows implementers to incorporate Dublin Core records for harvesting by Open Archives Initiative (OAI) search engines. OAI hopes to build an international database that will permit free access to scholarly articles and other materials via the Internet. As set forth in their mission statement, 'The Open

Archives Initiative develops and promotes interoperability standards that aim to facilitate the efficient dissemination of content' (Open Archives Initiative, year unknown). Awareness of these efforts and the standards that emerge are essential for anyone involved in digital publishing. The more we can agree upon standards and adhere to them, the closer we can come to fulfilling the dream of a global digital library.

Standards are not the answer to all our problems, however; like everything else, they have their limits. The biggest problem can be summed up in the saying, 'The nice thing about standards is that there are so many to choose from'. Which standards are we using, and how are we using them? The answer to this question will inevitably differ from institution to institution and from discipline to discipline. There will have to be more discussion and involvement by librarians, archivists and other guardians of cultural heritage in an international effort to agree on which standards to use and how to implement them. In the meantime, it is important that the metadata for all your digital files document what standard, and which version of the standard, was used, such as TEI P5.

How standards are implemented can vary as widely as which standards are used. Limitations on resources – time, money, personnel, expertise – will influence how well an institution adheres to standards. The quality of metadata, especially, depends on who creates it. An experienced cataloguer will generally do a better job than a student intern with one day of training. At the other extreme, 'the great is the enemy of the good': excessive devotion to perfection in standards can lead to a very limited number of digital objects, but with impeccable metadata, meeting very exact standards. However, is this sort of perfection the best use of our resources and the main goal of our efforts? The greater good would arguably be served by larger digital collections that are somewhat less than perfect. Standards can be a delicate balancing act: while one must not become so devoted to keeping perfectly to the ideal that production is severely diminished, one must resist the pressure to *get it online now* – that leads to sloppy work and neglect of necessary standards. We must strive for the golden mean, implementing standards at an appropriate level for our institution's resources and doing so consistently. As my instructor in a Text Encoding Initiative training course once said, 'If you can't be right, at least be consistent'. Standards like Dublin Core, TEI and EAD were designed to be flexible to meet the needs of a wide variety of materials and institutions, and this flexibility can be both a blessing and a curse. One may be tempted, especially when using XML-based standards, to make changes or to indulge in what is called 'tag abuse' – using XML mark-up in a way that is not intended by the schema or document type definition (DTD). As it is very simple to make changes to a DTD, it is all too easy to resolve a problem with mark-up by modifying the DTD to suit your purposes. However, this defeats the very purpose of standards. I have had the experience of having to deal with a digital collection that had been digitised by a vendor, who assured the institution that the documents would be marked up according to the Text Encoding Initiative Guidelines, using the TEI DTD. Unfortunately, this is not what the vendor did, as I discovered when I tried to use Perl scripts written for TEI-encoded documents on these files. The TEI DTD had been modified by the vendor, and the mark-up was not compliant with the TEI standard, making interoperability with a properly encoded TEI collection impossible. Consequently, the mark-up had to be redone in-house, a great waste of time and resources. This was an early lesson to me in the importance of adhering to standards.

Standards not only have to be chosen and followed, they have to be maintained. We have a professional duty, set forth in every code of ethics for the information professions that I have encountered, to keep abreast of new developments in our field, and for digital librarians this means keeping up with standards. Standards are not set in stone; they are changed and upgraded as technology progresses. The original TEI and EAD mark-up was in SGML; both are now XML. XML is far easier to work with than SGML, and facilitates interoperability and software development. This change has required institutions with SGML TEI files to convert these files to XML. The standard for PDF files was first published in 2005, and it is to be expected that it too will evolve. Digital librarians must follow the work of the standards-making organisations: ISO, the TEI Consortium, W3C, and national standards organisations such as the Library of Congress or NISO in the USA and the British Standards Institution in the UK.

The best way to stay up to date on standards is to be active in professional organisations and to attend academic conferences that cover issues related to digital libraries. Get involved in organisations or library association subdivisions that are concerned with standards. Some librarians avoid serving on standards committees because the work is viewed as tedious, boring and bordering on obsessive compulsive. I'm not going to pretend that reading and commenting on proposed standards is thrilling work, but it is necessary and important work that we have an ethical obligation to undertake. A working group in the Society of American Archivists was instrumental in compiling and finalising the Encoded Archival Description standard, which is now maintained by the Library of Congress. Input from information professionals from a wide variety of institutions and backgrounds enriches the standard-writing process and brings the necessary expertise, insights and different perspective to the challenges that arise. Cooperation also increases the chances that the standard will emerge as one that meets the needs of many different organisations and one that is likely to be widely adopted and implemented. In order to bring about an interoperable global digital library that allows researchers to search digital collections from libraries, archives and museums worldwide without having to go to hundreds of different search sites, we must work together to devise and agree upon the standards for digital files and communications that will make this dream possible.

Resources

- Adobe Systems, TIFF Specification: *http://partners.adobe.com/public/developer/tiff/index.html*
- Dublin Core: *http://dublincore.org*
- Encoded Archival Description: *http://www.loc.gov/ead/*
- International Organization for Standardization (ISO): *http://www.iso.org*
- Joint Photographic Experts Group (JPEG): *http://www.jpeg.org/jpeg2000/index.html*
- Library of Congress, Standards: *http://www.loc.gov/standards/*
- National Information Standards Organization: *http://www.niso.org*
- Open Archives Initiative (OAI): *http://www.openarchives.org/*
- Text Encoding Initiative Consortium: *http://www.tei-c.org*
- World Wide Web Consortium: *http://www.w3c.org*

8

Ethics in the digitisation process

Materials have been selected, funding has been secured, and you are now ready to begin the actual work of digitisation. You now face ethical issues in determining who will do the work, what tools will be employed, how the work processes will be documented, and how the online publication will be presented.

Who will do the work?

There are two basic answers to this question, each raising its own set of ethical issues: you may choose to do the work in-house or to outsource it to another company or agency. In deciding whether or not to outsource the work, you must look at the resources you have available in-house. Academic institutions have the advantage of being able to hire students as part-time workers; other types of libraries, museums and archives must rely on regular staff and, possibly, interns. Can the work be done in-house without piling an impossible workload onto existing staff? Is there funding for additional or part-time workers? There is a fine line between maximising the efficiency of a small operation and exploiting workers. Academic institutions, especially those situated in smaller university towns with few other employment opportunities, can often attract student workers without having to pay more than minimum level wages. Often, university staff and faculty have little control over how much money can be paid to student workers, but they generally have some control over the working conditions. While my student workers' wages are set by institutional policy, I can provide other benefits to them that would not be available to them from part-time jobs in the private sector. Digitisation projects provide no public services that require set hours, so our flexible working hours have proved attractive to many student workers. In the Electronic Publishing Center at Oklahoma State University, we allow our students to set their own schedules; as long as they put in the agreed number of hours, generally 10–20 hours per week, we don't care when they do it. This relieves them from worrying about class schedules or needing to take off to study for an exam, and to some degree makes up for the relatively low wages they receive. Acquisition of skills with computers, software, XML and web design is another indirect benefit to student workers, allowing them to gain knowledge that might not be available from their academic courses. Whether we employ full-time staff or part-time workers in our in-house operations, we have an ethical obligation to treat these workers fairly and to avoid using the scarcity of our financial resources as a justification for exploiting or overworking people.

If you decide to outsource the work, try to learn as much as you can about the business practices of the companies you are considering. First, are they honest with their customers about the quality and quantity of the work to be performed? Ask for references from past customers and contact these people to check on their level of satisfaction with the company? Was the quality of the work up to their expectations and the company's promises? Was the work delivered on time? How would they rate the customer service they received? Also look at the online collections that were produced by the company. Does the company adhere to digital library standards and best practices? Unfortunately, there are companies that will take advantage of inexperienced customers by passing off an inferior product as meeting prevailing standards and practices. To protect yourself from unscrupulous operators it is important to be educated about standards and processes even if you do not plan to do the work in-house. Outsourcing does not relieve you of concern with the questions of who will perform the work and where it will be done. Many digitisation operations keep their costs down by sending work 'offshore' to a country with low wages and few labour regulations, where their workers are forced to accept working conditions and wages that would be completely unacceptable to most of us. You do have an ethical duty to enquire into the treatment of the company's workers; choosing to remain ignorant of their labour practices does not relieve you of being morally culpable for the exploitation of the workers. There are companies that have overseas operations that, while they are run less expensively than would be possible in more developed countries, do treat their employees fairly and indeed offer opportunities that would not otherwise be available to the population. Take the ethical responsibility of finding out with whom you are dealing.

A good way to protect yourself, your institution and your ethics when outsourcing digitisation work is to get it in writing. I'm sure it seems that this is my answer to everything, but quite often written agreements are our best friends. Some institutions require that you get bids on any outsourced project; if your employer has such a requirement, you will need to write a Request for Proposal (RFP), setting forth the tasks to be accomplished and spelling out any restrictions, such as time limits, standards to be met, and adherence to fair labour practices. Even if you do not have to put the job out for bid, it is a good idea to write an RFP or some type of project descriptions to spell out what you expect from a vendor. This is an opportunity to clarify the tasks to be accomplished and to set a precedent for clear communication between you and the vendor. When you have chosen a company to do the work, there should be some sort of contract or other written commitment recording your agreement.

What tools will you use?

If you undertake the project in-house, you will need to select the appropriate hardware and software. Software has a tendency to lead even the most ethical into temptation because it is so easy to violate software licences, rationalising that it's so expensive, you're a cash-strapped non-profit, and Bill Gates doesn't need the money anyway. This sort of behaviour, in addition to being illegal, is unethical. You are putting your organisation in danger of severe legal penalties by using unlicensed software, including fines and seizure of property. You risk your own professional career. And, as your mother taught you, stealing is wrong, and unlicensed use of software *is* stealing. If you have four computers, you buy four software licenses. If you can't afford licences for all of the software you need for all of your computers, designate different machines for different tasks – the machine with PhotoShop™ is used for image editing; another, with OmniPage™, is used to OCR text. If you are having trouble finding enough money to pay for all of the software licences you need, there are alternatives to illegal copying. Contact the manufacturer of the software and enquire about discounts for multiple licences or special pricing for educational or non-profit institutions. We had priced a software package online and found that we could not afford the licences we needed. When we contacted the company to ask if we could get a discount, as we are a non-profit educational institution, we received a price that was a fraction of the retail price. Do not be deterred by the list price for software; frequently you can get a discount if you ask for one. Inability to pay retail for software is no justification for unlicensed use; there are legal and ethical alternatives.

One of the great money-saving tools for operations on a budget is shareware, software developed by a small company or independent programmer and made available online. Shareware works on the honour system: the user may download and use the software for free, and then pay for it if they like it. The fee is usually quite low, in comparison with commercial software, but it is quite simple to avoid paying for the software without fear of legal repercussions. This would be unethical not only because it would be stealing someone else's intellectual property, but because it would discourage the ingenuity and innovation of these programmers who offer an inexpensive alternative to commercial software packages. If you do try shareware and decide to keep using it, make the ethical choice of paying the fee indicated in order to support these innovative individuals and companies.

Documenting workflow and practices

Metadata for digital objects should always contain information about their creation. We have an ethical obligation to document our collections sufficiently so that someone who was not involved in their creation will be able to manage the collection effectively. Administrative metadata should tell the reader when, where, and by whom the work was created. The metadata should specify the version of the software used to create the file, explain file-naming protocols and any ID numbering systems, and identify any controlled vocabularies and encoding schemes used – things future administrators would need to know. Most metadata formats have a 'notes' field, where you can explain the rationale for any decisions that might not be obvious. Documentation, if done properly, will allow another professional to come in with no prior knowledge of your project, to determine what was done, how and why it was done, and to pick up the project where you left off. I try to make sure that my documentation is sufficient that, if I were hit by a bus, the project could be continued by someone else with minimal disruption. None of us will be in our jobs forever, and we must plan for the future not only by creating files that meet current standards but by documenting them so that our successors will be able to migrate, update and refresh the files as needed. It will do no good to create preservation-quality digital files if we do not also leave behind the information necessary to maintain them.

Presenting the collection online

The final step in the digitisation process is publishing the digital files on the Web. In designing the Web presence for our collections, we have an ethical duty to consider accessibility from two perspectives: (1) that of the physically challenged, and (2) that of the user with a low-bandwidth connection. The World Wide Web Consortium (W3C) Web Accessibility Initiative (WAI) has published guidelines for making websites accessible (W3C, 2005d). WAI also offers information about evaluation, repair, and transformation tools that can assist web content developers with designing accessible sites (W3C, 2005e). You can check online to see if your website is compliant with the Americans with Disabilities Act 1990 by using Watchfire's free software WebXACT (*http://Webxact.watchfire.com/*). However, reading guidelines and running utilities to confirm accessibility is not the same as trying to navigate a site yourself with a special browser like that used by the blind. WAI also offers you the opportunity to put yourself in the place of a disabled user by downloading a free trial or demonstration of alternative browsing methods (W3C, 2005f). I recommend trying an alternative browser, and if you are unable to do that, try navigating your website without using your mouse. It will open your eyes to the challenges faced by users with disabilities, and it is easier to treat others as you would want to be treated in their place if you actually put yourself in their place. Field test your web pages in these alternative browsers and see how well they perform in real life, as opposed to in accessibility testing software. If you find it confusing, someone who is not the designer and cannot see will find it more so. If you get tired trying to navigate your website using the arrow keys, imagine the fatigue of a quadriplegic who must do so with a mouth-held pointer. It is all very well to pay lip service to accessibility, but until you have experienced the Web from the alternative point of view, you will not appreciate the real importance of the issue.

Designing for low bandwidth can actually be more challenging because rarely will you have the opportunity to test your site over a dial-up connection. Most of the institutions that host digital libraries have high speed broadband connections, and increasingly home Internet connections are cable or DSL lines rather than telephone lines. We are all used to having Macromedia Flash™ presentations and large PDF files load quickly into our browsers. However, not all of our users will be so lucky. In many areas around the world, particularly in more isolated rural areas where laying fibre-optic cable isn't cost effective for the businesses involved, the old 56K modem connections over wire telephone lines provide the only available access, even in libraries and schools. This poses a problem for web content developers, particularly those dealing with multimedia files or PDF publications. At my institution, we have chosen to forego impressive graphics and multimedia presentations in favour of making our web pages more accessible to all users, including those with low bandwidth connections. As we specialise in digitising print materials, we have had to find ways to make those files in PDF format small enough to download in a reasonable amount of time. I still recall the frustration of waiting for large files to download over dial-up connections, something that could take an hour or more – and that was successful only if I didn't lose that fragile connection at some point during the process, only to have to begin it all over again; I would never want to inflict that situation on anyone. If a PDF file of a complete publication would be a prohibitively large file, we will break it down into smaller chunks – articles, cases, chapters – so that the files will be of a manageable size. In the case of both XML files and PDF files, it may be better to put derivative files on the website rather than the preservation version that meets all of the requirements of the respective standards. Just as we use GIF or JPEG derivatives rather than the large TIFF image files, so we can use HTML and smaller, compressed PDF files on our websites, maintaining the XML and PDF/A versions in the archive on our server. Theoretically, XML files can be converted to HTML with style sheets in more recent versions of Internet Explorer and Mozilla Firefox, but many users do not upgrade their browsers regularly and may be using a version that is several releases behind the current one. In order to reach the widest possible audience, we convert our XML files to HTML before uploading them to our website. In the end, the question to ask yourself is, 'Will this design allow *anyone* with an Internet connection and a browser – of whatever kind – to use my site?' You will not end up with the most beautiful, interactive, award-winning site if you answer that question 'Yes', but you will have the comfort of knowing that your digital collections are as accessible as you can possibly make them and that you have faithfully followed the codes of ethics for the information professions that exhort us to facilitate access for all users.

9

Ethics and digital preservation

Librarians have long been the guardians of knowledge, striving to collect, protect, and preserve the intellectual output of civilisation. This role is one that we must continue to pursue in the digital age. One of the main ethical principles set forth by the Charted Institute for Library and Information Professionals is 'Concern for the conservation and preservation of our information heritage in all formats'. Often librarians become so focused on access that they forget or simply neglect preservation, but without preservation there will be nothing to access, especially in this digital age. Digital preservation is far more complex than paper preservation: one must take into consideration hardware, software, storage media and file formats, as well as content. A word processing document in Wordstar format stored on a 5.25-inch floppy disk is an excellent example of digital obsolescence. A professor at my university brought his 1980s dissertation to the Electronic Publishing Center (EPC) in this format, requesting that we migrate the file to a Word file. We had no hardware that could accommodate his obsolete storage media, no software that would open a Wordstar file and no way to access the content. We ended up acquiring a paper copy of the dissertation, scanning it and converting it to an ASCII text file with Optical Character Recognition software. This example illustrates the vulnerability of digital materials as opposed to those printed on paper. Libraries and archives contain ancient papyri, illuminated medieval manuscripts, and Gutenberg-printed books, all of which can still be accessed, although we might find the script or language difficult to decipher. A 20-year-old electronic file on a floppy disk is unreadable if we do not have access to the hardware and software used to create it. When CD-ROM became a popular storage media, the popular joke in the information technology community was 'it lasts forever or five years, whichever comes first'. Now we could probably change that to two years, given the rapid rate of changes in computer technology. Planning and implementing digital preservation systems is an important ethical obligation for digital librarians.

A digital preservation system ideally will ensure 'that the information it contains remains accessible to users over a long period of time' (Rosenthal et al., 2005). As Rosenthal and colleagues (2005) observe in the article 'Requirements of Digital Preservation Systems', the problem is that the 'long period of time' over which the information will be needed far surpasses the lifespan of the hardware, software, storage media and file formats involved. They caution those planning for digital preservation to 'anticipate failures and obsolescence' and to guard against them by designing a system with no single point of failure, with diversity in its components, planned replacements of hardware, software and media as they become obsolete, and regular audits to check accessibility of files.

Digital objects that need to be preserved may be divided into two classes: those that were created by your institution and that are not held elsewhere, and those created by others that may be held in a number of institutions. Electronic journal subscriptions and government publications fall into the second category. The first group, the digital objects unique to your institution, must receive top priority in your preservation efforts because you have the sole responsibility for maintaining them. As in every other area, resources for digital preservation are scarce and a certain amount of triage will take place. You may not want or be able to preserve every version of your digital files, so you must decide which ones are to be kept for the long term.

There are a number of threats to digital collections that digitisation planning must take into account: media failure, hardware failure, software failure, network problems, media and hardware obsolescence, software obsolescence, human error, natural disaster, attack by hackers, lack of funds and demise of the hosting institution (Rosenthal et al., 2005). It is part of a digital librarian's professional duty to be aware of these menaces and to have a plan to protect against them and to recover from them. One of the great advantages of digital files is the ease with which they may be copied, and one of the best methods of protecting digital information is through replication, the technical term for making copies. There should *always* be more than one copy of the digital files you plan to preserve. Failure to back-up these critical files is negligent in the extreme, and a breach of professional ethics. It is best to have copies of the files in different locations to avoid catastrophic loss in case of natural or man-made disaster. One of the pioneering programmes in digital preservation, LOCKSS (Lots of Copies Keep Stuff Safe), is based upon maintaining multiple copies of digital files in geographically diverse institutions (*http://www.lockss.org*). The LOCKSS system was developed at Stanford University in the USA, and now includes over 100 libraries around the world. To explain it very simply, libraries participating in LOCKSS back-up each others' digital collections over an open source peer-to-peer network. Whether the problem is a minor network glitch that temporarily interrupts access to electronic journals or the catastrophic destruction of a library's technology infrastructure, the LOCKSS system will ensure that the library's patrons have continued access to its electronic collections. The LOCKSS Alliance has negotiated terms with publishers that will allow member libraries to maintain digital copies of the journals to which they subscribe electronically (a problem that will be discussed more fully in Chapter 11) and is working on a pilot project with the US Government Printing Office to preserve electronically published US government documents.

Government documents are an essential source of information on many topics, including not only laws and regulations, but census data, demographics, statistics on social and economic issues, ecological reports, patents and agricultural information. Increasingly, more and more countries are publishing government-produced information in electronic formats only. The primary reasons for converting to electronic publication are economy of production and ease of access, but there are serious downsides. First, there is the ease with which digital files can be altered or removed by the government, and the possibility of governments restricting access to information that was once freely available or tracking the identity of those who access it. In the USA, government documents are, by law, deposited in designated libraries around the country to ensure both access by citizens in all geographic areas and preservation via what Thomas Jefferson called a 'multiplication of copies, as shall place them beyond the reach of accident'. Electronic government publications are vulnerable to all of the aforementioned threats and more. Production of these digital publications is often delegated to individual agencies or departments, without specifications for standard file formats or metadata, and without planning for the maintenance of the files. Depository libraries that formerly received copies of every government publication do not receive physical copies or copies of the electronic files, which are stored on servers administered by the government agencies. In the past few years, since September 11, 2001, some publications have disappeared, withdrawn by the US government for 'national security' reasons. The removal of these documents did not require the recall of dozens of printed materials from depository libraries; it was accomplished by deleting the files from a web server. This sort of centralised and exclusive control of information is chilling to citizens' rights of access, and permits abuse of the management of information that the depository library system was designed to prevent. GODORT, the Government Documents Round Table of the American Library Association (*http://sunsite.berkeley.edu/GODORT/*), is an organisation of librarians working in depository libraries who are committed to free and equitable access to government information for all citizens. They have formed a Task Force on Permanent Public Access to Government Information to examine issues of the removal of or restrictions on access to government documents and the archiving of digital information. As stated in their final report (GODORT, 2003):

> The issue of greatest concern for this work group in terms of archiving federal government information is the archiving and perpetual usability of 'born digital' information originating from agencies or hosted on the Government Printing Office (GPO) servers.

The report recommends a cooperative approach to archiving by depository libraries, to be coordinated by the Government Printing Office (GPO):

> [E]ach depository should be able to archive the key documents and reports of an office at a minimum even if it is only keeping the copies on a CD or zip drive. It may

be possible that regional libraries or large depository libraries with server space will freely host information while the smaller depositories aid in archiving.

Here is an excellent example of librarians living up to the ideals set forth in our codes of professional ethics and undertaking to ensure ongoing access to and preservation of digital collections.

Standards also play a role in digital preservation programs, most notably the Open Archival Information System (OAIS) standard, ISO 14721:2003 (OAIS, year unknown), which defines an archive reference model and describes the components and participants in such a model. The Research Libraries Group (RLG) and OCLC have built on the OAIS model to develop the concept of trusted digital repositories: 'A trusted digital repository is one whose mission is to provide reliable, long-term access to managed digital resources to its designated community, now and in the future' (RLG-OCLC, 2002). They continue (RLG-OCLC, 2002: 5) by saying that to be designated as a trusted digital repository, an electronic archive must:

- accept responsibility for the long-term maintenance of digital resources on behalf of its depositors and for the benefit of current and future users;

- have an organisational system that supports not only long-term viability of the repository, but also the digital information for which it has responsibility;

- demonstrate fiscal responsibility and sustainability;

- design its system(s) in accordance with commonly accepted conventions and standards to ensure the ongoing management, access and security of materials deposited within it;

- establish methodologies for system evaluation that meet community expectations of trustworthiness;

- be depended upon to carry out its long-term responsibilities to depositors and users openly and explicitly;

- have policies, practices, and performance that can be audited and measured; and

- meet the responsibilities detailed in Section 3 of this paper [covering the areas of the scope of collections, preservation and lifecycle management, the wide range of stakeholders, copyright and ownership of materials, and cost implications].

A trusted digital repository complies with the Reference Model for an Open Archival Information System (OAIS) and demonstrates administrative responsibility, organisational viability, financial sustainability, technological and procedural suitability, system security and procedural accountability (Ibid.:13). The very name 'trusted digital repository' implies a fiduciary duty and ethical obligation; those who deposit items into such a digital preservation system are *trusting* that the operating entity will live up to its promises to keep the information safe and accessible over the long term. There will likely be some degree of competition among institutions to be declared 'trusted digital repositories' and an accompanying temptation to perhaps exaggerate or overestimate the capability to fulfil the necessary requirements in order to persuade would-be depositors and to win support and funding. It is important to take the idea of *trust* and all that this implies very seriously when reviewing one's ability to undertake such a commitment. It is an ethical obligation of the highest order and is not to be taken lightly.

The importance of disaster planning has been highlighted by the calamitous events of recent years, including terrorist attacks, tsunamis, hurricanes, floods and earthquakes. We all have a duty to plan for the natural disasters to which our geographic locations are prone, and we must remember that human attack – whether from bombs or computer worms – and human operator error are threats to which everyone is vulnerable regardless of their location. Loss of information seems inconsequential in comparison with loss of human life, but it is collateral damage in any disaster. In August 2005, levees protecting the city of New Orleans, Louisiana, failed in the wake of hurricane Katrina, flooding large portions of the city and surrounding communities. Real estate transactions became impossible in the wake of the disaster, because the paper documents needed to complete title searches were water-logged when the basement of the courthouse where they were stored flooded (Thomas, 2005). Computerised records were available only for records filed after 1985. The benefits of having computer files backed up in a different location were immediately evident in the days following the flood, as firms with branch offices and back-up computer servers in unaffected areas were able to proceed with little information loss. The state of Oklahoma, where my institution is located, is in 'Tornado Alley', a section of the USA especially prone to tornadoes and violent wind storms. To prevent losing our computer files to such threats, we store a back-up copy of our digital collections on CDs in an underground bank vault located in a different city than Oklahoma State University. Even if the EPC is flattened by an F5 tornado, our digital collections can be restored. Consider the threats to your building and its contents and plan accordingly. Replication of your digital files, with back-up copies on a variety of storage media kept in geographically diverse locations, is a simple and effective method of protecting your digital objects from disaster.

There is one obstacle to development of better digital preservation systems that all of us can do something about: not allowing others to learn from our mistakes.

> To improve the performance of systems over time, it is essential that lessons be learned from incidents that risk or cause data loss ... Past incidents suggest that an institution's reaction to data loss is typically to cover it up, preventing the lessons from being learned. (Rosenthal et al., 2005)

It is very appealing to write an article or make a presentation at a professional conference telling our colleagues how we did something well; it is much harder to tell a wider audience how things went wrong. However, we have an ethical duty to the greater good of digital preservation to share the lessons we've learned the hard way. One of the most frightening and the most useful presentations I've ever attended was given by an employee of the National Museum of the American Indian, who related the series of errors that led up to the failure of the museum's new storage area network resulting in the loss of terabytes of data (Sledge, 2003). The museum looked to their archival DVDs to restore the lost data, only to discover that a change in DVD technology since the time the copies were made caused a problem in retrieving the data. Fortunately, they were able to find a work-around solution and restore the lost files, and thanks to Ms Sledge's courage in admitting she and her colleagues had made mistakes we can all learn a lesson about the importance of backing up our data and of migrating our archival copies to new storage media as technology changes. I had a similar experience with our digital collection at Oklahoma State University. When files were being moved to a new server, something went wrong and a gigabyte of our data was lost. I was under the impression that the library systems department was backing up the server every night, and that it would be a simple matter of retrieving the data from the back-up tapes. Alas, it was not so. Systems did a complete back-up every 30 days, but it had been several weeks since the server in question had been completely backed up. Systems was forced to look to the campus IT department's daily back-ups and to painstakingly retrieve our server files from the daily campus-wide back-up tape for each day of those past weeks. Even with those efforts, we still lost some files that had to be redone. This incident made me and the rest of the EPC staff aware of the inadequacy of our back-up procedures. It was not enough to look to others to do our back-up for us; we must institute a policy of backing up our own work every night to a computer in the EPC. This procedure is now a part of our workflow. Additionally, we burn DVDs of our collection every two months and store them in the offsite vault described earlier. If you experience a digital preservation problem, share the lessons learned with your colleagues. Perhaps in this way, we can all avoid making the same mistakes.

A great online 'public good' is the Internet Archive (*http://www.archive.org/*), founded by Brewster Kahle in 1996 'to build an "Internet library", with the purpose of offering permanent access for researchers, historians, and scholars to historical collections that exist in digital format' (*http://www.archive.org/about/about.php*). Kahle, inventor of the Wide Area Information Servers system, is concerned about a 'Digital Dark Age' caused by the disappearance of born-digital materials and is contributing his time, intellect and money to the cause of preserving our digital history. Using the Internet Archive's Wayback Machine, searchers can type in a URL and find all previous versions of that website. By maintaining a historical record of the Internet, the Internet Archive strives to fulfil its goal: 'Universal access to human knowledge'.

10

Ethics and access

'Information wants to be free.' This statement, made by Stewart Brand (1985), has been a credo of the Internet since its very beginning. Brand is a computer scientist, not a librarian, but his statement is also a long-held tenet of the library profession. Librarians have a deep-rooted 'commitment to the defence, and the advancement, of access to information, ideas and works of the imagination' (CILIP, 2004). A comparative analysis of codes of ethics of library associations in 34 countries revealed that one of the almost universally embraced principles is 'the principle of free access to information' (Trushina, 2004). '[E]ven allowing for all the differences in cultural traditions and development trends in different countries ... the right of free access to information is proclaimed as a basic aim of library activities' (Ibid.: 417).

Open access

In his book *The Media Lab: Inventing the Future at MIT*, Stewart Brand states:

Information Wants To Be Free. Information also wants to be expensive. Information wants to be free because it has become so cheap to distribute, copy, and recombine – too cheap to meter. It wants to be expensive because it can be immeasurably valuable to the recipient. That tension will not go away. It leads to endless wrenching debate about price, copyright, 'intellectual property', the moral rightness of casual distribution, because each round of new devices makes the tension worse, not better. (Brand, 1987: 202)

The tension over free or expensive information has only increased since 1987, and nowhere is this more evident than in scholarly publishing. Journal prices have risen astronomically; the expenditures by research libraries on journal subscriptions rose by 227 per cent in North America and 158 per cent in the UK in the last decade of the twentieth century (ARL, 2004). Libraries were forced to cancel some subscriptions, to the consternation of affected faculty, because their budgets could not keep up with price increases. Anger at the traditional scholarly publishing system – wherein faculty in pursuit of tenure *must* publish, and thus provide their writings to journal publishers for no compensation, only to have these publishers package the scholars' writings into journals the research libraries at the scholars' institutions can't afford – boiled over, and the open access movement was born. In the best tradition of utilitarian ethics, open access proponents would combine the willingness of scholars to make their research available to others for no payment with the ability of Internet technology to make information freely available to everyone for a great public good. This was set forth in the Budapest Open Access Initiative (2002) as follows:

The public good they make possible is the world-wide electronic distribution of the peer-reviewed journal literature and completely free and unrestricted access to it by all scientists, scholars, teachers, students, and other curious minds. Removing access barriers to this literature will accelerate research, enrich education, share the learning of the rich with the poor and the poor with the rich, make this literature as useful as it can be, and lay the foundation for uniting humanity in a common intellectual conversation and quest for knowledge.

In addition to providing users with 'extraordinary power to find and make use of relevant literature', the great good of open access 'gives authors and their works vast and measurable new visibility, readership, and impact' (Ibid.). Libraries are leading the way in the open access movement. SPARC (Scholarly Publishing and Academic Resources Coalition) and SPARC Europe are alliances of libraries formed in response to rising costs of academic journals 'to unleash the potential of the digital networked environment for enhancing the scholarly communication process' (SPARC, 2004). SPARC advocates change in the 'system and culture of scholarly communication' (Ibid.) through its Create Change programme (*http://www.createchange.org*). The Create Change programme encourages public advocacy for open access and is complemented by the Declaring Independence initiative that seeks to empower libraries to become electronic publishers. Implementing open access primarily takes two forms: publishing alternative free peer-reviewed journals and depositing copies of journal articles in digital institutional repositories where they can be found and freely accessed via Internet search. SPARC encourages libraries to become publishers of open access journals and to host institutional repositories.

Institutional repositories

Institutional repositories, also known as digital repositories or digital archives, are defined in a SPARC position paper as 'digital collections capturing and preserving the intellectual output of a single or multi-university community' (Crow, 2002). Faculty and researchers at universities deposit digital copies of their articles, conference papers, research sets, working papers and course materials into a centrally managed electronic archive. For some time now, individual researchers and faculty members have put their writings online via their personal websites, but until recently there were no efforts to systematically collect all of the intellectual output of a university. Libraries, as the traditional collectors of knowledge for university communities, have a leading role to play in implementing institutional repositories; this requires cooperation from a number of stakeholders. '[A]n effective institutional repository of necessity represents a collaboration among librarians, information technologists, archives and records mangers, faculty, and university administrators and policymakers' (Lynch, 2003). According to Crow (2002), the institutional repository can help to fulfil the traditional functions of scholarly communication through:

- *registration* – establishing the intellectual priority of an idea, concept, or research;

- *certification* – certifying the quality of the research and/ or the validity of the claimed finding;

- *awareness* – ensuring the dissemination and accessibility of research, providing a means by which researchers can become aware of new research; and

- *archiving* – preserving the intellectual heritage for future use.

Metadata for the materials in these repositories will be harvested by special search engines, allowing scholars to search the contents of repositories around the world from a single portal. The Open Archives Initiative (OAI), not to be confused with the Open Access Initiative, aims to facilitate interoperability between repositories. The term 'OAI-compliant' designates institutional repositories' software solutions and metadata that meet the specifications set by OAI for interoperability. If you are planning an institutional repository, look for software and choose metadata formats that are OAI-compliant. When an institutional repository is OAI-compliant, its metadata are exposed to OAI metadata harvesters that collect from institutional repositories around the world, making metadata available for scholars to search.

Ethical decision making for institutional repositories will include considering standards, formats and preservation issues discussed in previous chapters and additional questions in the area of intellectual property and access. If an article by a faculty member has been or will be published in a non-open access journal, it will be necessary to determine the institution's right to make it freely available in an institutional repository. SHERPA (Securing a Hybrid Environment for Research Preservation and Access, *http://www.sherpa.ac.uk/*), is a UK-based project to develop open access institutional repositories in research universities. SHERPA maintains a database, called ROMEO, of the archiving policies of various journals and publishers (*http://www.sherpa.ac.uk/romeo.php*). SHERPA also offers advice and guidance on creating institutional repositories, advocacy on open access issues, submission of materials, preservation, and licensing policies. If submissions to the institutional repository are not published elsewhere, librarians can encourage faculty and researchers to use a Creative Commons licence (*http://creativecommons.org/*) that preserves their copyright but allows free access and use for educational or research purposes.

There are four stakeholders in any institutional repository: authors, publishers, users and the institution itself. The librarians who maintain the institutional repository have ethical responsibilities to all parties. Institutional repositories are an excellent way to fulfil our professional duty to facilitate access to information for our users, but we also have a responsibility to ensure that the contents of the institutional repository are of the calibre researchers would expect of a scholarly journal or institution. There must be some parameters on what will be accepted by the institutional repository; users must be able to trust the content we provide. Authors should not be misled about the benefits and risks of contributing to institutional repositories. The benefits are quite rightly extolled by open access proponents, but the risks are rarely mentioned. Probably the greatest risk to the author and the institution is the premature publication of research that might lead to a patent. Patent laws are very strict about *any* prior publication of the contents of a patent application, and all faculty should be directed to clear their submissions with the university's research office to make sure they are not making public any research that might be part of a subsequent patent submission. While this prohibition does hinder the free flow of scientific ideas, the reality is that many universities depend on income from patents resulting from faculty research, and it would be irresponsible for the library to sabotage that revenue stream by publishing a paper before the related patent applications have been filed. It is a good idea to have the university's research office involved in the planning of the institutional repository, and to have an institutional repository policy (again, get it in writing!) that outlines what items may be contributed to the institutional repository, identifying the parties in academic departments or in the research office who must receive approval before a file is deposited in the digital archive. The wider exposure afforded by making research available in an institutional repository does increase the risk that work will be stolen or used without attribution; there is no way to assure a scholar absolutely that their work will not be misused. While most would agree that the benefits of making scholarly research more widely available outweigh the risks posed by open access, authors have the right to be fully informed of both sides of the story. Librarians owe an ethical duty both to publishers and to their institutions to respect copyrights and to honour the publisher's policy regarding deposit of articles in institutional repositories. There is a duty to the authors, the institution and the users to maintain the technological infrastructure of the institutional repository and its contents in order to ensure ongoing accessibility. SPARC offers guidelines and checklists for institutional repositories (Crow, 2002), and the Digital Library Federation provides the 'Digital Repository Summary Checklist of Service Requirements, with Recommended Best Practices' (Blinco, 2004), an easy-to-follow outline of the essential, desired and optional services that digital repositories should offer. As always, following best practices and standards is the ethical thing to do.

Open access journals

BioMed Central (*http://www.biomedcentral.com/*), is an example of the alternative publishing model. BioMed provides open access to dozens of peer-reviewed journals in the biological sciences. Of course, nothing is completely free; there are still publication costs that must be covered, and the BioMed model does this by assessing a flat article-processing charge for publication. These fees, which range from a low of £330/€480/$585 to a high of £950/€1380/ $1690 depending on the journal, are paid by the authors or their institutions. Some grant-making agencies will allow these publishing expenses to be covered by grant funds, and there is a campaign underway to get more funding agencies to support such activities. Libraries have the opportunity to play a key role both in publishing open access journals and in promoting their acceptance by the scholarly community. The open access publishing model will never take hold if faculty cannot be assured that an article published in an open access journal will be given the same weight as a traditional peer-reviewed print journal when senior faculty and administration are deciding whether to grant tenure to the author. Librarians can and should take an active role in educating faculty and administration about the open access movement and the new scholarly publishing paradigm. There are strong utilitarian ethics arguments for open access; it clearly is a case of the greatest good for the greatest number. The benefits of open access publishing to the scholarly community as a whole are great public goods. It facilitates discourse among researchers by reducing the long lag times before research is published in a print journal and by broadening the scope of articles available. There is also the matter of money saved on traditional journal subscriptions and overcoming the limitations on accessible materials caused by budgetary concerns. If a library decides to participate in publishing an open access journal, the librarians assume a new ethical duty: a responsibility for the accuracy and quality of the content that was hitherto borne by the publishers. In selecting journals for their libraries, librarians have always relied on the experience and reputation of the editors and publishers of journals to determine the quality and authenticity of the contents. In the open access model, editors and peer reviewers will still be an essential part of the process, and their expertise will determine the content, but the library, as publisher, must also accept responsibility for the materials they put out into the scholarly realm. Care in selecting what open access journals the library should publish becomes an ethical duty for electronic publishing librarians.

Resisting censorship and protecting patron privacy

The Open Access movement and institutional repositories are proactive ways digital librarians can improve access to information and promote the free flow of ideas, but there are also battles to fight against censorship and other restrictions on intellectual freedom and virtually all professional codes for information professionals call on us to 'resist all efforts to censor library resources' (ALA, 1995). In a recent survey, nearly 20 per cent of those responding felt that censorship was no impediment to access to information for their patrons (Miltenoff and Hauptman, 2005), yet even in democracies where freedom of speech is a cherished tradition, we continue to see efforts to censor library materials, including government documents, children's books and Internet access.

At one time, librarians were expected to provide information to anyone who asked for it, without regard to whether that information might be used for nefarious purposes. If a patron used information accessed with the help of a librarian to poison someone, the librarian would have no moral responsibility for this; they had merely fulfilled the professional duty to provide equal access to information for all. I came to librarianship from the legal profession, and the ethical duty to provide information without considering the morality of doing so reminded me very much of the lawyer's duty to represent his or her client zealously, regardless of whether the party was innocent or guilty. However, as Miltenoff and Hauptman (2005) observe:

> This attitude was irresponsible and slowly eroded so that now, although philosophical conflicts still do exist within librarianship, many practitioners are willing to take ethical responsibility for their actions and may refuse to help or provide information, if it appears that it will lead to horrific consequences.

Two things seem to have profoundly impacted this change in attitude: the advent of the Internet, which made information that would never have been included in a libraries collection, such as child pornography, easily accessible from library computers, and the terrorist attacks of September 11, 2001, which heightened awareness of the incredibly evil uses to which information and electronic communications could be put. A librarian's 'higher allegiance to society and humanity' (Ibid.) was recognised as trumping the professional ethic of providing access to information in a morally neutral manner. This does not, however, mean that librarians should give in to efforts to censor materials; every attempt to block access to information should be questioned and examined to determine whether it is a legitimate effort to prevent a greater harm to society or an effort to impose the political or religious agenda of one group on society as a whole. Those responsible for encroachments on access to information usually try to justify their actions by claiming threats to national security or dangers to children from inappropriate materials. Sometimes these claims and restrictions are justified; no one wants terrorists obtaining blueprints for nuclear facilities or paedophiles using the library's computers to obtain child pornography. My European colleagues are always shocked to hear of the efforts by religious conservatives to ban certain materials from libraries, but this is a situation that American librarians face daily. As I write this, the Legislature of my state, Oklahoma, is considering several bills that would place restrictions on access to materials in public libraries and that would penalise libraries by withholding funding from any who dare to defy these efforts at censorship. We face such situations over the question of filtering Internet access, over books and other materials with homosexual themes, and over such 'satanic' materials as the *Harry Potter* books. When librarians resist such efforts, we are painted as everything from traitors to pornographers. American librarians are certainly not alone; many of our colleagues around the world face much harsher government or religious interference with the free flow of ideas. Currently, there is controversy about the decision of Internet search engines Google and Yahoo to comply with the Chinese government's demands that they filter search results returned to Chinese citizens. The search engines are commercial concerns; for them this concession is the price of doing business in China. To librarians, however, the idea of filtering the search results returned to our users is discomfiting if not unethical. I have seen librarians from oppressed nations speak out bravely at international conferences, letting their colleagues from around the world know the truth of their situations in hopes that we could raise consciousness of the problem in our home countries. Librarians, whether working in digital or traditional settings, cannot turn to professional codes of conduct for a quick and easy answer to questions of the ethical dilemma of providing access to information that may be harmful to the individual or to society. As Irina Trushina (2004: 418) noted in her article, 'Freedom of access: ethical dilemmas for Internet librarians':

On the one hand, libraries must respect the principle of intellectual freedom as their institutional mission. Indeed, libraries were established with the aim to preserve and distribute information. On the other hand, library functions are human targeted, and librarians, like physicians or teachers, are morally responsible to their users. A librarian should respect both public morals and human life.

An issue closely related to freedom of access is respect for patron's confidentiality. Trushina (2004) found that these two concerns were the key aspects of library associations' professional codes of ethics, regardless of the country of origin. She also observes that 'American librarians are known for the most radical professional attitudes' (Ibid.: 418). The ALA Code of Ethics proclaims, 'We protect each library user's right to privacy and confidentiality with respect to information sought or received and resources consulted, borrowed, acquired or transmitted', while the UK CILIP Ethical Principles more moderately urge 'Respect for confidentiality and privacy in dealing with information users'. While many international codes of ethics specify that librarians will protect patron privacy unless the law requires them to reveal the information, the ALA code gives US librarians no such out. Consequently, many librarians have engaged in civil disobedience of a sort, destroying electronic records of patrons' use of library materials that might be subject to seizure by warrant or subpoena. An October 2003 e-mail written by a Federal Bureau of Investigation (FBI) agent decried the 'radical, militant librarians' whose opposition to the USA PATRIOT Act 2001 was preventing law enforcement from obtaining access to library users' records. It is a label the ALA has proudly embraced. American librarians who have reported suspicions about patrons to law enforcement have been widely condemned by their colleagues. Miltenoff and Hauptman (2005) cite the case of a Florida librarian who contacted the FBI after September 11 with information about one of the suspected terrorists. While some people praised her actions, others condemned her violation of professional ethics. A case study discussed at the 2005 meeting of the Society of American Archivists (SAA) related the story of an archivist who suspected that a patron might be a paedophile, based on the information requested by this person. Against the orders of a supervisor the archivist reported these suspicions to the police, and was fired for doing so. The panellists for the case study, archivists from historical societies, a corporation and a university, all agreed that the person who broke patron confidentiality and went to the police had behaved in an unprofessional and unethical manner and was properly terminated. They also observed that being fired for such an action would render the person practically unemployable in the archives world. Personally, I felt sympathy for the fired archivist; I don't think I could have lived with the fear that my failure to speak up might have resulted in a child being irreparably harmed. The knowledge that I had adhered to a code of professional ethics would be cold comfort indeed. There will always be some situations when there is a conflict between personal ethics and professional ethics, and in those situations the librarian involved can only follow their own conscience.

11

Ethics and digital library management

Digital librarians not only have to contend with ethical decisions in creating and preserving electronic resources, they also have to incorporate the business ethics of managing people and resources, negotiating contracts or licences, and avoiding bias and conflicts of interest in their professional lives. In this chapter we will examine these responsibilities and the associated ethical dilemmas.

Personnel management

Many digital librarians will also be managers of other professionals and staff. The ALA Code of Ethics states, 'We treat co-workers and other colleagues with respect, fairness and good faith, and advocate conditions of employment that safeguard the rights and welfare of all employees of our institutions'. The CILIP Code of Professional Practice goes into more detail, instructing members to:

2. afford respect and understanding to other colleagues and professionals and acknowledge their ideas, contributions and work, wherever and whenever appropriate;

3. refer to colleagues in a professional manner and not discredit or criticise their work unreasonably or inappropriately;

4. when working in an independent capacity, conduct their business in a professional manner that respects the legitimate rights and interests of others;

5. encourage colleagues, especially those for whom they have a line-management responsibility, to maintain and enhance their professional knowledge and competence.

The codes of ethics for information professionals I examined are unanimous in urging respect for co-workers, and encouragement of their continuing education. In this they differ from the codes of conduct of other professionals – those for the legal and medical professions, for example, make no provision for treatment of colleagues or employees (e.g. American Bar Association Model Code of Professional Conduct, *http://www.abanet.org/cpr/mrpc/mrpc_toc.html*, and American Medial Association Principles of Medical Ethics, *http://www.ama-assn.org/ama/pub/category/2512.html*). The library profession has always emphasised personal relationships – between librarians and clients and between co-workers. This emphasis cannot change in the computer age; quality information services still depend upon 'people skills': the ability to communicate, understand and relate well to others.

Information professionals have an ethical duty to ensure the competence of staff and subordinates by supporting training and continuing education; further, a number of ethics codes urge members to provide encouragement to those who are interested in becoming librarians or information professionals. Libraries are facing a 'greying of the profession problem': librarians, especially those in administrative and managerial positions, are reaching retirement age and there are not enough qualified professionals to take their place in library leadership. In recognition of this shortage of information professionals, the US Institute of Library and Museum Services has instituted a new grant programme to educate 'Librarians for the 21st Century' (*http:// www.imls.gov/applicants/grants/21centuryLibrarian.shtm*). Ask librarians why they decided on their line of work, and most will mention a librarian who made an impression on them when they were young – something that few professionals other than physicians or teachers can claim. Members of the profession have a duty to, as the ALA Code of Ethics puts it, 'foster ... the aspirations of potential members of the profession'. Our codes of conduct also direct us to represent the profession well, to 'act in ways that promote the profession positively' (CILIP, 2004).

As managers, digital librarians also have a responsibility to ensure that those who work for us are treated and compensated fairly. Staff positions in libraries are often seriously underpaid, and many library workers are forced to supplement their income with part-time jobs. I believe that as supervisors, we have an ethical duty to fight for adequate and equitable compensation and benefits for our staff. We must educate personnel officers about the specialised skills required for digital library staff, the enormous and valuable contributions made by these workers, and the levels of compensation and professional respect that are their proper due. Too often, there is a view that any ten-year-old can design a website or operate a scanner. This fallacy must be exposed, and our administrations must be made aware of how difficult it really is to design a navigable, accessible website, to operate the delicate high-end scanners used in digital library operations, and to produce high-quality images, searchable PDF documents, and valid, well-formed XML files. Digital librarians must take every opportunity to raise awareness of the high levels of technical skills, knowledge of standards, and attention to detail possessed by digital library workers. Digitisation staff spend more time on continuing education than many information professionals, due to ever-evolving software and hardware and the rapidity of change in the field. While they may not possess advanced professional degrees, they are highly trained professionals in their own right. They deserve to be paid accordingly and to be treated with respect by administrators, librarians, IT professionals and vendors. It is part of a manager's job to insist that they are. One of the 12 Ethical Principles underlying the CILIP Code of Conduct calls for '[r]espect for the skills and competences of all others, whether information professionals or information users, employers or colleagues'. Following this advice will serve all digital librarians well in personnel matters. Everyone has a contribution to make to the success of the library, from the person reshelving books to the worker scanning documents to the dean or head of library services, and all deserve respect for the roles that they play.

Dealing with vendors

Managing a library's digital resources will involve working with vendors to negotiate licences and contracts for databases and software, purchasing big-ticket items such as high-end scanners, and ensuring that our institutions get their money's worth. The digital environment has made management of subscriptions far more complicated than in the past, when serials librarians dealt with print journals, when vendors provided a middleman for dealing with publishers, and when old issues of journals were bound and kept in the library's collection; the biggest problem with ongoing access to back issues was running out of space in which to store old bound journals. All this has changed as more and more journals have gone to print and electronic or electronic-only publishing, and since users now demand that resources be accessible outside the four walls of the library, 24 hours a day, and that they be keyword-searchable. Databases of electronic journals are governed by licensing, and libraries purchase only *access* to the information contained therein, not the information itself. In the past, if we cancelled a subscription to a print journal, that simply meant we would receive no future issues; back issues we had received under the subscription were ours to keep and use forever. Not so with subscriptions to databases and electronic journals; in most cases, access to future *and* past issues ceases with the cancellation of a subscription. Even in cases where the library keeps a subscription to a database service, they are dependent on the publisher or database provider to maintain the digital archive of older material. This is a matter of great concern to academic libraries, and more and more research libraries are insisting on a right to maintain their own back-up copies of electronic journals. This matter must be discussed in the licence negotiations, and an arrangement for back-up of databases must be reflected in the licence agreement; otherwise the library could be in violation of copyright laws and subject to civil and criminal sanctions. When I attended library school in the 1990s, there was little discussion of licence negotiations. Now, this subject *must* be covered in preparatory courses. Librarians who will have responsibility in these areas could certainly benefit from business law courses and training in the techniques of negotiations. Fostering good relationships with vendors and publishers can be helpful in this regard. It is not good to go into the negotiating process viewing the vendor/publisher as an enemy; whatever we may believe about the fairness of their pricing, they still supply a product the public needs, and they have a right and a need to make money in order to stay in business. It is best to work toward a deal that benefits both parties. For example, pointing out that allowing a LOCKSS-type back-up of databases and electronic journals relieves the publisher of the onerous burden of providing the sole digital archive for this valuable information can make the idea more attractive than fulminating about the unfairness of pricing schemes and access policies. This argument also happens to be true – something that is essential for any negotiating technique. In addressing 'business relationships', the Code of Ethics for the American Association of Law Libraries (AALL) states, 'We promote fair and ethical trade practices', and 'We strive to obtain the maximum value for our institution's fiscal resources, while at the same time making judicious, analytical and rational use of our institution's information resources'. Fulfilling these duties as well as the CILIP Code of Conduct's admonition to 'defend the legitimate needs and interests of information users, while upholding the moral and legal rights of the creators and distributors of intellectual property', requires that we serve the interests of our employers and users while still dealing ethically and forthrightly with vendors. When negotiating agreements, the chief user/employer interests that must be protected are the right to back-up copies for ongoing access and the right for authors to deposit copies of their work in institutional repositories. Of course, access to the most information possible for the least amount of money is the ultimate goal, but this objective must be achieved through careful research into the options available and through fair and ethical dealings – never via shortcuts or methods that would compromise our professional ethics, intellectual property laws or our institution's integrity.

Digital librarians may also be responsible for purchasing major equipment, including scanners, servers, and high-powered computer workstations, as well as specialised items like digital cameras, digital video equipment and specialist software packages. In these instances, we have an ethical duty to do our research and find the best possible deal for our employers, as the codes quoted above indicate. For very high-priced items, we may need to develop requests for proposals (RFPs) and put them out for bid. There are not-for-profit library service agencies, like Amigos Library Services in the USA, that can help librarians write RFPs. It would be a good idea to seek out their services or to get help from colleagues who have experience in this area. RFPs can be difficult to write, and you owe it to yourself and your institution to make sure your request for bids covers everything you will need the equipment to do. The good thing about RFPs, despite the labour involved in writing them, is that they remove any suspicion of favouritism from the selection process. All sorts of rumours and suspicions arise with the purchase of expensive items, and it is important to avoid even the appearance of impropriety. Vendors will invite librarians whose job it is to recommend purchases out for business lunches or dinners, and will otherwise court those who might buy their projects. They are sales people, and up to a point this is their job. Obviously, if someone offers you a bribe or kickback to recommend purchasing their product, such an overture is definitely unethical and probably illegal. But where to draw the line in what you accept from vendors? Library conferences would not happen without vendors; their sponsorship and exhibits make our meetings possible. It in no way compromises your integrity to attend the conferences they sponsor, to enjoy the receptions they have catered or to take a pen, paperweight or other free 'swag' from their booths. For one thing, there is safety in numbers, and these events are being staged for the benefit of all the librarians who attend, not just those who make purchasing decisions. These events also allow you to get to know vendors and their products in an atmosphere where there is no pressure to buy and no concentrated focus on you. Outside of conferences the situation becomes more questionable. One librarian made it a rule not to accept meals from vendors from whom he had not purchased anything; that way, if he subsequently made a purchase, he could be sure he hadn't been influenced by any favours he had accepted from the vendor (Presley, 1993). However, Presley also points out that it isn't a good idea to solve the ethical dilemma by simply avoiding business lunches entirely; they can be important opportunities to learn from colleagues. He prefers occasions that involve librarians from other institutions and offer networking opportunities (Ibid.). Where then do you draw the line in accepting gifts or favours from vendors? The IEEE Code of Ethics provides guidance for engineers in these matters, advising them 'to avoid real or perceived conflicts of interest whenever possible' and 'to reject bribery in all its forms'. Grupe (2003) advises asking yourself 'Would I be embarrassed if others knew what I am doing? Would other professionals accept my actions as being neutral and defensible?' If the answers to these questions are 'yes' or 'no', respectively, or if you feel any impulse to keep what you are considering doing from your employer or colleagues, it is a good indication that you probably should not do it. It is not a bad idea to run something by your boss if you think there may be some question as to whether you would be putting yourself in an inappropriate situation. If you work for a government agency or state institution, there may be ethics rules for employees that will indicate what is and is not acceptable behaviour for employees. Make sure you are aware of and follow any such directives.

The Caux Round Table is an international organisation that promotes ethical business practices and socially responsible capitalism. They have promulgated Principles for Business Ethics for dealing with vendors (Caux, 1994) that are excellent guidelines to follow:

> Our relationship with suppliers and subcontractors must be based on mutual respect. We therefore have a responsibility to:
>
> - seek fairness and truthfulness in all our activities, including pricing, licensing, and rights to sell;
>
> - ensure that our business activities are free from coercion and unnecessary litigation;
>
> - foster long-term stability in the supplier relationship in return for value, quality, competitiveness and reliability;
>
> - share information with suppliers and integrate them into our planning processes;
>
> - pay suppliers on time and in accordance with agreed terms of trade; and
>
> - seek, encourage and prefer suppliers and subcontractors whose employment practices respect human dignity.

Conflicts of interest

Ethicists have identified seven types of conflicts of interest: self-dealing, accepting benefits, influence peddling, using your employer's property for private advantage, using confidential information, outside employment (or moonlighting), and post-employment conflict of interest

(Grupe, 2003). *Self-dealing* is defined as 'a situation in which you capitalise on your position for personal gain' (Ibid.). This would cover situations in which you directed business to an outside company in which you are a stockholder or hired a relative or friend for a position when other candidates were more qualified. *Accepting benefits* is the more straightforward, and illegal, taking of cash or other bribes in return for a certain action. The long-term 'loan' of software or equipment from a vendor for one's personal use would also fall under this category. *Influence peddling* is a sort of you-scratch-my-back-I'll-scratch-yours ethical conflict usually associated with politicians and lobbyists, but it can apply to information professionals as well. If you give your business to a vendor who then recommends you as a consultant to his other customers, you are engaging in this sort of activity. *Using your employer's property for private advantage* is a very obvious and very common conflict of interest *if you are doing this for personal gain and/or without your employer's knowledge or consent.* Running your own digitisation business using your institution's scanners and software is definitely an unethical conflict of interest. On the other hand, I am writing this book on a computer owned by my employer, using software licensed to the university. The difference is that research and writing is considered a part of my job, and my employer is aware of this activity and has given permission for it. *Using confidential information* can become an issue if you use insider, confidential knowledge gained through your employment to further your own interests. Insider trading is the most infamous example. *Outside employment and moonlighting* frequently becomes an issue for those with in-demand technical knowledge and skills. Faculty have long supplemented their meagre academic salaries by acting as consultants or paid experts to other organisations. It is important to make sure any outside activity does not assist a competitor of your organisation, does not take place on your employer's time, and is fully disclosed to and approved by your employer. *Post-employment conflicts* can arise when an information professional leaves one organisation to take a similar position with another. This situation is bound to occur in most of our professional lives, and when it does we have an ethical duty not to make the mistake of blurring our ownership of intellectual property or trade secrets with that of our former employer. If, for example, you developed database software for your previous employer, you do not have the right to implement that same software for your new employer without licensing it from your former employer. It doesn't matter that *you* came up with the software; you were paid to do so by your former employer and they own the rights to it. If you wish to use it in your new position, you must arrange to license it from your former employer.

Grupe (2003) suggests three methods of dealing with these ethical dilemmas: managing, escaping or disclosing. *Managing* involves the employer putting rules and procedures in place, so that employees are on notice as to what behaviour is considered a conflict and how situations that arise should be handled. Some organisations will have a compliance officer or committee to deal with these issues. *Escaping* does not involve running off to an island in the Caribbean, tempting as that may be. It refers to removing yourself from a decision when you have an outside interest in one of the parties concerned that might be perceived as affecting your decision. It is the equivalent of a judge recusing him- or herself from ruling in a case that involves a company in which the judge has an interest. *Disclosure* is your best defence in any situation and will usually be a part of any attempt to reconcile a conflict of interest. Most universities require faculty who are applying for funding or grants to sign a disclosure statement setting forth any financial interests they may have in outside parties. Telling your employer what you are doing, whether it is consulting for another institution or writing a book on a company computer, is always the best policy. It demonstrates your good faith and your honesty. And, as noted above, if you're doing something you would not want your employer to know about, you probably shouldn't be doing it. If you are approached by a vendor or other outside party with an offer that you think ethically questionable, the quickest way to defuse the situation and to avoid any hint of wrongdoing is to report the matter to your employer. Don't make the mistake of trying to handle something by yourself; this can backfire and give the appearance of your being involved, at least to the extent of trying to cover up improper behaviour. To hold the respect and trust of our colleagues, we must be, like Caesar's wife, above reproach.

Bias

Bias is the most insidious of ethical problems, because it can affect our behaviour without our being aware of it. Most of us, as educated individuals, would consider ourselves unbiased as to someone's race, creed, gender or sexual orientation. These characteristics have no bearing on the person's abilities to perform their duties, whether as an employee, vendor or outsourcer and we would vigorously deny that these facts had any bearing whatsoever on our decisions. As it turns out, however, we would be wrong. We are suffering from what psychologist David Armor has termed the 'illusion of objectivity' (Banaji et al., 2003). We have *implicit,* or unconsciously held, biases that are quite contrary to our explicit or consciously held beliefs. These implicit biases arise from stereotypes that we buy into without even being aware of it, due most likely to the human brain's need to categorise and associate like things. To test yourself, check out the Implicit Association Test (IAT) at *https:// implicit.harvard.edu/implicit/demo/*. This online test requires you to respond quickly to words flashed on the screen as being either good or bad. These negative words are interspersed with pictures or words describing two groups, such as blacks and whites. The idea is that you will unconsciously classify the group against which you have an implicit bias by hitting the same button you would hit for the negative concepts. You will likely be surprised at your results. Becoming aware of our unconscious biases is the first step in reducing the effect they have on our decision making.

Researchers also find that while we may not discriminate against people who are different from us, we often show a marked preference for people who are like us. How many times, in search committee meetings, have you heard someone remark on a candidate's ability to 'fit in'? We wonder if we would be comfortable working with a person, based on their personality, lifestyle, and way of communicating. This is natural, but it is also dangerous. An overly homogeneous workplace can be one in which no one 'thinks outside the box'. We need a wide variety of people on our teams who can contribute the ideas and attitudes that come from different backgrounds and experiences of the world. It's rather like yin and yang: we need the balance brought about by differences.

How can we eliminate, or at least reduce the biases that affect our decisions? First, by becoming aware of them using the IAT or a similar tool. Next, we should make an effort to challenge the stereotypes we hold by broadening our exposure to different representations of other groups and social environments. Researchers have found that biases can be considerably reduced by exposing subjects to a non-stereotypical representation of an ethnic group (Banaji, 2003). Positive images and experiences have an impact on our implicit biases. One method of removing bias from the decision-making process is by using what John Rawls called the 'veil of ignorance', the concept that 'only a person ignorant of his own identity is capable of a truly ethical decision' (Ibid.). This follows Kant's thinking that the only purely good act is one which affords you no benefit at all. When making the decision, try to imagine you are someone else, perhaps by putting yourself in the shoes of those in whose interests you are supposed to be acting. If you were the user or client for whose benefit we make digital resources available, what decision would you make? If you were an auditor of your institution what would you do? If asked to 'show your work' as we were on maths quizzes in school, would your thought process in making this decision seem logical, legitimate and ethical to a reasonable person? These considerations can help you to look at the situation with more objectivity and to make a better, more unbiased decision.

12

Ethics for twenty-first century librarians

What then must we do? (Leo Tolstoy)

The world has changed dramatically since the first professional code of ethics for information professionals, that of the American Library Association, was formulated in 1938. While the professional societies have updated their codes from time to time, they haven't focused much on ethics since the advent of the Internet, the Web and digital resources changed not only the way we do our jobs but the way we live our lives. While librarians have definitely been on the frontlines fighting for free speech and for access to information for all, there is a certain complacency in the matter of professional ethics. Few graduate programmes in information science offer courses that focus solely on information ethics, few professional conferences or seminars include ethics as a component of the subjects covered, and few professional organisations require annual continuing education in ethics, as is the case for other professionals. The International Center for Information Ethics (*http://icie.zkm.de/research*) differentiates between ethics, morals and laws as follows:

- morals: customs and traditions;

- ethics: critical reflection on morals;

- law: norms formally approved by state power or international political bodies.

It seems that librarians and other information professionals are falling behind in the field of ethics, in that there is little critical reflection on the customs and traditions (morals) of our profession in light of the changes in the world around us. The most immediate concerns of librarians in the information age revolve around the issues of access and confidentiality, and our codes of ethics already address these issues. Where the codes are woefully inadequate, in my opinion, is on the ethical issue of preservation. Rafael Capurro, founder of the International Center for Information Ethics and eminent scholar of information ethics, wrote in his seminal paper 'Ethical Challenges of the Information Society in the 21st Century' (Capurro, 2000: 264):

> The question of access cannot be separated from the question of sustainability. This is a big technical and *ethical* issue, particularly for the emerging digital libraries and archives that are committed to the preservation of cultural heritages in digital form. [Italics mine]

The Chartered Institute of Library and Information Professionals (CILIP) includes among its Ethical Principles 'Concern for the conservation and preservation of our information heritage *in all formats*' (italics mine), and its Code of Professional Practice lists 'show an appropriate concern for the future information needs of society through the long term preservation and conservation of materials as required, as well as an understanding of proper records management' as one of the Responsibilities to Information and its Users (*http://www.cilip.org.uk/professionalguidance/ethics/*). The CILIP website notes that the referenced page was updated on 3 February 2006, a fact that seems extremely relevant to its inclusion of the ethical concerns of digital librarians. Contrast this with the ALA Code of Ethics, adopted in and unchanged since 1995, which is completely silent on the subject of preservation. We cannot resolve twenty-first century ethical dilemmas with twentieth century codes of ethics. We have a responsibility to society, to our profession and to ourselves to reflect upon and to address the ethical issues of the information age.

As technology has been developed, humans have evolved from an oral tradition to a written and then a printed one, and now to networked society. Consequently, ethical concerns have moved from freedom of speech to freedom of the press and now to freedom of access (Capurro, 2000). Freedom of access is a global issue with many facets. In the past decade, the freedom of access concerns of the profession have grown in scope from local to global. We are no longer merely concerned with Internet connectivity in our own schools and libraries or with fights over filtering Internet access. Now we are concerned about the digital divide between rich and poor in our own countries, the difficulties of accessing the Internet in developing or war-torn nations and the state-ordered censorship of the Internet by China, the world's most populous nation. 'The dichotomy between information-rich and information-poor countries, and links between information access and economic wellbeing, are matters of concern for us all' (Hannabuss, 1998). In the 'digital cosmos' we are all, like Diogenes, 'citizens of the world' (Capurro, 2000). What are our ethical obligations in the networked world? According to information and computer ethicist Luciano Floridi (1998), 'information welfare ought to be promoted by extending (information quantity), improving (information quality) and enriching (information variety) the infosphere'. These activities are very much the job of digital librarians. Our efforts to make more resources available online, to ensure the quality of the materials we digitise, and to make a wide variety of digital resources available all support this dictum, which Floridi calls the highest moral law in information ethics. If we ever had any doubts about the importance and significance of our work, this emphasis on extending, improving and enriching access should eliminate them.

Where should we look for inspiration in revising our codes of professional ethics? The works of Rafael Capurro and Luciano Floridi are an excellent place to begin with the theoretical underpinnings of information ethics. For guidance in applied ethics, we can look to the ethical codes of computer professionals, such as those of the Institute of Electrical and Electronic Engineers (IEEE) and the Association of Computing Machinery (ACM). The IEEE Code of Ethics states:

We, the members of the IEEE, in recognition of the importance of our technologies in affecting the quality of life throughout the world, and in accepting a personal obligation to our profession, its members and the communities we serve, do hereby commit ourselves to the highest ethical and professional conduct and agree:

1. to accept responsibility in making engineering decisions consistent with the safety, health and welfare of the public, and to disclose promptly factors that might endanger the public or the environment;

2. to avoid real or perceived conflicts of interest whenever possible, and to disclose them to affected parties when they do exist;

3. to be honest and realistic in stating claims or estimates based on available data;

4. to reject bribery in all its forms;

5. to improve the understanding of technology, its appropriate application, and potential consequences;

6. to maintain and improve our technical competence and to undertake technological tasks for others only if qualified by training or experience, or after full disclosure of pertinent limitations;

7. to seek, accept, and offer honest criticism of technical work, to acknowledge and correct errors, and to credit properly the contributions of others;

8. to treat fairly all persons regardless of such factors as race, religion, gender, disability, age, or national origin;

9. to avoid injuring others, their property, reputation, or employment by false or malicious action;

10. to assist colleagues and co-workers in their professional development and to support them in following this code of ethics.

This code's recognition of the effect its members can have on the global community would be very appropriate for librarians in the digital age. As we move beyond managing print collections in local libraries to publishing digital materials for a global audience, our actions have more impact than ever before. Consequently our actions have the potential to do more harm, or more good, than ever before. Our ethical obligation to be competent is more important than ever. As Hannabuss (1998) observed, 'For professional people, their profession is not merely a way of making a living: it is carrying out an occupation or vocation with which standards of competence and responsibility are associated'. The IEEE emphasis on qualifications, continuing training, and constructive criticism reflects the strong ethos of competence in the professional. The ACM Code of Ethics and Professional

Conduct (ACM, 1992) includes 'general moral imperatives' to 'contribute to society and human well-being' and 'avoid harm to others' as well as 'professional responsibilities' to:

- strive to achieve the highest quality, effectiveness and dignity in both the process and products of professional work;

- acquire and maintain professional competence;

- know and respect existing laws pertaining to professional work;

- accept and provide appropriate professional review;

- give comprehensive and thorough evaluations of computer systems and their impacts, including analysis of possible risks;

- honour contracts, agreements, and assigned responsibilities;

- improve public understanding of computing and its consequences;

- access computing and communication resources only when authorised to do so.

The commentary on the code states, 'Excellence is perhaps the most important obligation of a professional. The computing professional must strive to achieve quality and to be cognisant of the serious negative consequences that may result from poor quality in a system'. Both the IEEE and ACM Codes acknowledge that professionals with specialised technical knowledge have a heightened duty of care towards those who, due to their lack of expertise and/ or dependence on these services, are at their mercy. In the words of Robert F. Kennedy (1965), 'The problem of power is how to achieve its responsible use rather than its irresponsible and indulgent use'.

Beyond the moral and ethical, there is a legal reason to strive for the highest levels of competence: information liability and negligence (Hannabuss, 1998). This new and sobering concern is especially relevant for those of us who live in litigious societies. If we are professionals whose competence may be assumed, we must expect to be held accountable if we perform our duties negligently and cause harm to others. Such negligence becomes even more of a concern when we are the publishers of information that turns out to be wrong. In the past, librarians never expected to be the targets of a lawsuit if they botched a reference search – for one thing, we never made enough money to make us attractive targets. If, however, we post inaccurate information on our institution's website, the institution could be liable, providing the 'deep pocket' of funds for potential damages that trial lawyers often seek. The possibility of a lawsuit has been a concern for me personally, because two of my major projects have involved the digitisation of legal materials. Our first digitisation project was *Indian Affairs: Laws and Treaties,* a compilation of the legal materials governing relations between the Native American Indian tribes and the US government. We made the decision to put JPEG images of the actual pages of the law books online in addition to the digitised text. Although we had proofread our text, which had been rendered by optical character recognition and marked up in XML, we were still concerned about accuracy. A single error could completely change the meaning of a statute; a party who relied on that information in a court case or contract negotiation could suffer considerable damage due to our mistake and could, in turn, sue us. By making the actual page images available, we protected both ourselves and our users from any inadvertent error in the text. Our subsequent legal project, *Decision of the Indian Claims Commission*, was published in searchable PDF format, basically allowing the user to use the books themselves online.

What then must we do, in this new world of digital librarianship, to live up to the core values of our profession? First, we must educate those entering the profession in information ethics. The International Center for Information Ethics (*http://icie.zkm.de/research*) proposes the following educational goals:

- to be able to recognise and articulate ethical conflicts in the information field;

- to activate the sense of responsibility with regard to the consequences of individual and collective interactions in the information field;

- to improve the qualification for intercultural dialogue on the basis of the recognition of different kinds of information cultures and values;

- to provide basic knowledge about ethical theories and concepts and about their relevance in everyday information work.

Our schools of library and information science should consider these goals when planning their curricula for twenty-first century librarians. Next, we should update our codes of professional ethics to address the ethical dilemmas of digital librarians. And, of course, we should adhere to these codes of conduct. In the end though, I believe we come back to Aristotle's theory of virtue: the question is not 'what should we do?' but 'what should we be?' *Modus operandi sequitur modum essendi*: action follows being (Capurro, 2000). If we reflect on our morals and behave as persons of principle, we will be the ethical professionals we want to be.

Bibliography

American Library Association (1953–2004) 'Freedom to read statement'. Adopted 25 June 1953; revised 28 January 1972, 16 January 1991, 12 July 2000, 30 June 2004, by the ALA Council and the AAP Freedom to Read Committee. Available online: *http://www.ala.org/ala/oif/statementspols/ftrstatement/freedomreadstatement.htm* (last accessed: 15 March 2006).

American Library Association (1995) 'Code of ethics' (revised 28 June). Available online: *http://www.ala.org/ala/oif/statementspols/codeofethics/codeethics.htm* (last accessed: 15 March 2006).

American Society for Information Science and Technology (1992) 'ASIS&T professional guidelines'. Available online: *http://www.asis.org/AboutASIS/professionalguidelines.html* (last accessed: 15 March 2006).

Aristotle 'Nicomachean ethics', in McKeon, R. (ed.), Ross, W. D. (tr.) (1992) *Introduction to Aristotle*. New York: The Modern Library.

Association des Bibliothécaires Français (2003) 'Le code de déontologie du bibliothécaire de L'Association des Bibliothécaires Français' translated by Marie-Hélène Maynard. Available online: *http://www.ifla.org/faife/ethics/frcode-e.htm* (last accessed: 15 March 2006).

Association for Computing Machinery (1992) 'ACM code

of ethics and professional conduct'. Available online: *http://www.acm.org/constitution/code.html* (last accessed: 15 March 2006).

Association of Research Libraries (2004) 'ARL statistics'. Available online: *http://fisher.lib.virginia.edu/arl/index.html*.

Banaji, M. R., Bazerman M. and Chugh, D. (2003) 'How (un)ethical are you?', *Harvard Business Review* 81(12): 56–64.

Blinco, K. (2004) 'Digital repository summary checklist of service requirements, with recommended best practices'. Washington, DC: Digital Library Federation. Available online: *http://www.diglib.org/pubs/cmsdl0407/cmsdl0407check.htm* (last accessed: 15 March 2006).

Brand, S. (1985) 'Transcript of 1984 Hackers' Conference', *Whole Earth Review* 46 (May): 49.

Brand, S. (1987) *The Media Lab: Inventing the Future at MIT.* New York: Viking.

Budapest Open Access Initiative (2002) Available online: *http://www.soros.org/openaccess/read.shtml* (last accessed: 15 March 2006).

Capurro, R. (2000) 'Ethical challenges of the information society in the twenty-first century'. *International Information & Library Review* 32: 257–76.

Caux Round Table (1994) 'Principles for Business Ethics'. Available online: *http://www.cauxroundtable.org/documents/Principles%20for%20Business.PDF* (last accessed: 15 March 2006).

Chartered Institute of Library and Information Professionals (CILIP) and Library Association Copyright Alliance (LACA) (year unknown) 'Copyright advice and guidance' Available online: *http://www.cilip.org.uk/professionalguidance/copyright/advice* (last accessed: 15 March 2006).

Chartered Institute of Library and Information Professionals

(2004) 'Ethical principles and code of professional practice for library and information professionals', updated 23 September. Available online: *http://www.cilip.org.uk/professionalguidance/ethics/* (last accessed: 15 March 2006).

Collaborative Digitisation Program (year unknown) 'Copyright & intellectual property resources' Available online: *http://www.cdpheritage.org/digital/legal.cfm* (last accessed: 15 March 2006).

Crow, R. (2002) 'The case for institutional repositories: A SPARC position paper'. Washington, DC: Scholarly Publishing & Academic Resources Coalition. Available online: *http://www.arl.org/sparc/IR/IR_Guide.html* (last accessed: 15 March 2006).

Dean, J. F. (2003) 'Digital imaging and conservation: model guidelines', *Library Trends* 52(1): 133–7.

Dublin Core Metadata Initiative (2003) 'Dublin Core metadata element set, Version 1.1: reference description'. Available online: *http://dublincore.org/documents/dces/* (last accessed: 15 March 2006).

Floridi, L. (1998) 'Information ethics: on the philosophical foundation of computer ethics', version 2.0. Available online: *http://www.wolfson.ox.ac.uk/~floridi/ie.htm* (last accessed: 15 March 2006).

GODORT (2003) 'Federal Documents Task Force On Permanent Public Access Final Report'. Available online: *http://tigger.uic.edu/~aquinn/access/final_report.pdf* (last accessed: 15 March 2006).

Grupe, F. (2003) 'Information system professionals and conflict of interest', *Information Management & Computer Security*, 11(1): 28–32.

Hannabuss, S. (1998) 'Information ethics: a contemporary challenge for professionals and the community'. *Library Review* 47(2): 91.

Harper, G. K. (2001) 'Crash course in copyright'. Available online: *http://www.utsystem.edu/ogc/intellectualproperty/cprtindx.htm* (last accessed: 15 March 2006).

Helig, J. (1999) 'Legal issues to consider when digitising collections'. Available online: *http://www.cdpheritage.org/digital/legalIssues.cfm* (last accessed: 15 March 2006).

Hirtle, P. (2006) 'Copyright term and the public domain in the United States'. Available online: *http://www.copyright.cornell.edu/training/Hirtle_Public_Domain.htm* (last accessed: 15 March 2006).

International Federation of Library Associations and Institutions (2005) 'Professional codes of ethics/conduct'. Available online: *http://www.ifla.org/faife/ethics/codes.htm* (last accessed: 15 March 2006).

International Organization for Standardization (2005) 'Overview of the ISO system'. Available online: *http://www.iso.org/iso/en/aboutiso/introduction/index.html* (last accessed: 15 March 2006).

Jones, R., Andrew, T. and MacColl, J. (2006) *The Institutional Repository*. Oxford: Chandos Publishing.

Kennedy, Robert F. (1965) 'I remember, I believe' in *The Pursuit of Justice*. London: H. Hamilton.

Lee, S. D. (2001) *Digital Imaging: A Practical Handbook*. New York: Neal-Schuman Publishers, Inc.

Library Association (1983) 'The Library Association's code of professional conduct'. Available online: *http://www.la-hq.org.uk/directory/about/conduct.html* (last accessed: 15 March 2006).

Lynch, C. A. (2003) 'Institutional repositories: essential infrastructure for scholarship in the digital age', *ARL Bimonthly Report* 226, p. 1. Available online: *http://www.arl.org/newsltr/226/ir.html*.

MacNeil, H. (1992) *Without Consent: The Ethics of Disclosing Personal Information in Public Archives*.

Metuchen, NJ: Society of American Archivists and Scarecrow Press.

Mautner, T. (ed.) (1999) *The Penguin Dictionary of Philosophy*. London: Penguin Books.

Mill, J. S. (1956) *On Liberty*. Indianapolis: Bobbs-Merrill.

Miltenoff, P. and Hauptman, R. (2005) 'Ethical dilemmas in libraries: an international perspective'. *The Electronic Library* 23(6): 664–70.

Morris, S. L. (2005) 'Preservation considerations for digitisation of archival materials', *Archival Outlook*, May/June, p. 9.

Murdock, D. (2005) 'Terror trove', *The Washington Times*, 24 April. Available online: *http://www.washingtontimes.com/commentary/20050423-104813-8475r.htm* (last accessed: 15 March 2006).

National Initiative for a Networked Cultural Heritage (2002) 'NINCH guide to good practice'. Available online: *http://www.nyu.edu/its/humanities/ninchguide/* (Version 1.0, last accessed: 15 March 2006).

National Library of Australia (year unknown) 'Digitisation policy, 2000–2004'. Available online: *http://www.nla.gov.au/policy/digitisation.html* (last accessed: 15 March 2006).

Open Archival Information System (year unknown) 'ISO 14721:2003' in: 'ISO Archiving Standards – Reference Model Papers'. Available online: *http://ssdoo.gsfc.nasa.gov/nost/isoas/ref_model.html* (last accessed: 15 March 2006).

Open Archives Initiative (year unknown) 'Mission statement'. Available online: *http://www.openarchives.org/organization/index.html* (last accessed: 15 March 2006).

Presley, R. L. (1993) 'Firing an old friend, painful decisions: the ethics between librarians and vendors'. *Library Acquisitions: Practice & Theory* 17: 53–9.

RLG-OCLC (2002) 'Trusted digital repositories: attributes

and responsibilities'. Available online: *http://www.rlg.org/ legacy/longterm/repositories.pdf* (last accessed: 15 March 2006).

Rosenthal, D. S. H., Robertson, T., Lipkis, T., Reich, V. and Morabito S. (2005) 'Requirements for digital preservation systems'. *D-Lib Magazine* 11(11). Available online: *http://www.dlib.org/dlib/november05/rosenthal/ 11rosenthal.html* (last accessed: 15 March 2006).

Ruethling, G. (2005) 'Almost all libraries offer free web access', *New York Times,* 24 June, p. A14.

Scholarly Publishing & Academic Resources Coalition (2004) 'Introducing SPARC'. Washington, DC: Association of Research Libraries.

Schrage, M. (1995) 'The rules of collaboration'. *Forbes ASAP Supplement.* 5 June: 88–9.

Schwartz, J. (2005) 'The archivist's balancing act', in Behrnd-Klodt, M.L. and Wosh, P.J. (eds) *Privacy and Confidentiality Perspectives: Archivists and Archival Record.,* Chicago: Society of American Archivists.

Sledge, J. (2003) 'Challenges in storing digital images' in *NINCH: Price of Digitisation Report.* Available online: *http://www.ninch.org/forum/price.report.html#js* (last accessed: 15 March 2006).

Society of American Archivists (1992) 'Code of ethics for archivists'. Available online: *http://www.archivists.org/ governance/handbook/app_ethics.asp* (last accessed: 15 March 2006).

Thomas, G. (2005) 'Wet records put house sales in limbo – Title searches, research come to a dead stop', *The Times-Picayune* (New Orleans, LA), 7 October, Metro section, p. 8.

Trushina, I. (2004) 'Freedom of access: ethical dilemmas for internet librarians', *The Electronic Library,* 22(5): 416–21.

UK Patent Office (year unknown) 'Copyright resources'. Available online: *http://www.intellectual-property.gov.uk/std/resources/copyright/index.htm* (last accessed: 15 March 2006).

Velasquez, M., Andre, C., Shanks, T. and Meyer, M. J. (1996) 'Thinking ethically: a framework for moral decision making', *Issues in Ethics* 7(1). Available online: *http://www.scu.edu/ethics/publications/iie/v7n1/thinking.html* (last accessed: 15 March 2006).

Waluchow, W. J. (2003) *The Dimensions of Ethics: An Introduction to Ethical Theory*. Ontario: Broadview Press.

World Intellectual Property Organization, 'Copyright and related rights' Available online: *http://www.wipo.int/copyright/en/index.html* (last accessed: 15 March 2006).

World Wide Web Consortium (W3C) (2005a) 'Web Accessibility Initiative'. Available online: *http://www.w3.org/WAI/* (Updated 12 September) (last accessed: 15 March 2006).

World Wide Web Consortium (W3C) (2005b) 'Web content accessibility guidelines (WCAG)'. Available online: *http://www.w3.org/WAI/intro/wcag.php* (Version 1.0) (last accessed: 15 March 2006).

World Wide Web Consortium (W3C) (2005c) 'Developing a web accessibility business case for your organisation'. Available online: *http://www.w3.org/WAI/bcase/Overview.html* (Version 1.0 Up-to-date as of August 2005) (last accessed: 15 March 2006).

World Wide Web Consortium (W3C) (2005d) 'WAI guidelines and techniques'. Available online: *http://www.w3.org/WAI/guid-tech* (last accessed: 15 March 2006).

World Wide Web Consortium (W3C) (2005e) 'Evaluation, repair, and transformation tools for web content accessibility'. Available online: *http://www.w3.org/WAI/ER/existingtools* (last accessed: 15 March 2006).

World Wide Web Consortium (W3C) (2005f) 'Alternative web browsing'. Available online: *http://www.w3.org/WAI/References/Browsing* (last accessed: 15 March 2006).

Index

Printed in the United Kingdom
by Lightning Source UK Ltd.
115581UKS00001B/33